SHORT BIKE RIDES ON CAPE COD, NANTUCKET & THE VINEYARD

Jane Griffith *and* Edwin Mullen

The Globe Pequot Press

Old Chester Road
Chester, Connecticut 06412

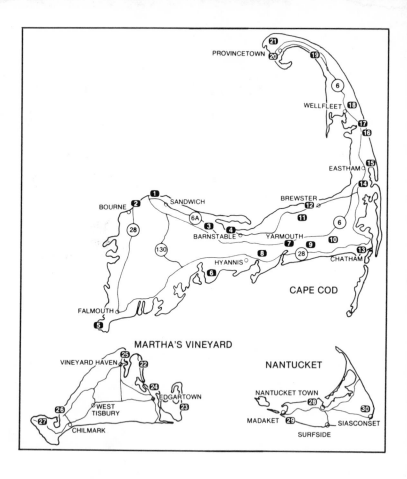

Contents

Introduction

These short rides provide an opportunity to explore Cape Cod and the islands in a unique and rewarding way: By bicycle on hassle-free, planned tours. The rides are from seven to twenty-seven miles long and range in difficulty from the flat terrain of the Cape Cod Canal to the hills of Martha's Vineyard. They can be ridden in a few hours, but to experience all the pleasures of the ride *allow at least* a half day. Don't let age deter you from taking these rides: We are forty-three and fifty-three, and children from age ten have also done the ride and had a good time. To ensure your enjoyment, take some precautions as outlined in the section on *Safety*, and some good equipment: For picnicking and swimming, pannier bags on your rear rack and handlebar bags are indispensable. As to the bike itself, we recommend a good ten speed model—the best you can afford. A three speed would be all right for the flat country rides but would take the enjoyment out of the others—and that's what it's all about.

Cape Cod

This arm of Massachusetts, site of the Pilgrims' first landfall, is about seventy-five miles long and has over three hundred miles of coastline. Formed some ten thousand years ago by action of the retreating glacier, the Cape is a bony, sandy outcropping punctuated by bluffs, marshes, and ponds (probably created when dense ice chunks amid the debris melted away).

The Cape was settled within a couple of decades of Plymouth, and the colonists took to fishing, hunting, and haying the salt meadows. Settlers also denuded the Cape of its trees for housing, ship building, firewood, and pasture land. The cutting over, combined with the natural wash and blow dry the flora and terrain absorb from relentless waves and winds, explains the Cape's unique and fascinating appearance: rugged but right.

Cape Cod National Seashore

The Cape Cod National Seashore was created in 1961 by Act of Congress. Its 27,000 acres located in six towns are under National Parks Service supervision. About two-thirds of the acres are owned by the Seashore; the rest of the acreage remains in private hands or is held by the towns, but physical changes to these properties are strictly controlled.

The two Visitors' Centers, Province Lands and Salt Pond, are open from 9:00–6:00, seven days a week, during the season. Salt Pond offers an illuminated table top map of the Cape, a brief introductory film, and dioramas illustrating the history and geology of the Cape, as well as trail guides and facilities. Province Lands Visitors' Center provides one of the Cape's most beautiful overlooks. Trail guides, exhibits, orientation talks, and facilities are available. Camping is not allowed in the Seashore. The dunes, flora and fauna must remain undisturbed. Lifeguard service and public facilities are available at the following beaches: Coast Guard, Nauset Light, Marconi, Head of Meadow, Race Point, and Herring Cove. The Seashore extends along the Cape's entire Atlantic shore, from its southernmost point below Chatham to Provincetown. Unforgettable!

Martha's Vineyard

In 1602, wild grapes grew abundantly on the Island, and in that year explorer Bartholomew Gosnold, who had a young daughter named Martha, took note of it, and made this vineyard, here on the other side of the world, her namesake.

Colonists came in 1642 to establish Edgartown, having bought the whole lashup, unbeknownst to the Indian inhabitants who had lived there compatibly time immemorial, for forty pounds from two gentlemen in England. The community prospered with fishing, whaling, sheep herding, dairying and boat building; new settlements were established. The Revolution disrupted the Islanders' lives and economy, but recovery was complete by 1820 when the whaling and building booms were at their height. The triple whammy of the Gold Rush, the Civil War and the discovery of petroleum would have resulted in a bleak future indeed had it not been for the timely burgeoning of summer religious camp meetings which prompted a land development boom. To this day tourism is the Island's principal source of income, causing the population to soar from some seven thousand year round residents to about seventy thousand in the season.

With that figure in mind, we exhort you not to bring a car here in the summer. Congestion is terrible and parking is ridiculous. From May through September: The bike's the thing! Bring your own, or rent one, and take the bus in between treks. (Shuttles operate back and forth from Vineyard Haven, Oak Bluffs and Edgartown twice an hour in season.) Ferries bring people to Vineyard Haven from Woods Hole and New Bedford, and to Oak Bluffs from Falmouth, Hyannis and New Bedford. No camping is allowed on the beaches. There are three commercial camp grounds. Oak Bluffs and Edgartown are wet; the rest of the Island is dry but you may bring your own. Beaches open to the public include (1) in Vineyard Haven: Owen Park Beach; (2) in Oak Bluffs: Joseph Sylvia State Beach, and the Town Beach; (3) in Edgartown: Katama (South) Beach; (4) in Chappaquiddick: East Beach; (5) in Chilmark: Menemsha Town Beach and Menemsha Hills; (6) in Gay Head: Lobsterville Beach. The Martha's Vineyard State Forest Bike Trail provides the cyclist with fourteen miles of bike paths around and through this four thousand acre pine, oak and spruce forest. A good starting point is the Youth Hostel on the West Tisbury Rd. As the forest is smack in the middle of Martha's Vineyard, however, all roads lead there! You can pick up a map of the Trail anywhere on the Island.

Nantucket

Nantucket, thirty miles south of Cape Cod, was created when a glacier melted away dropping the immense load of earth and debris which shaped the Island's width and length of three miles by fifteen.

Martha's Vineyard's discoverer Gosnold also came here in 1602, but the Island wasn't settled until some sixty years later when the Quakers came. The Indians were kindly disposed— which was apparently unfortunate for them: By the middle 1800s they had left or died off and their culture vanished from Nantucket.

From 1712, when the first sperm whale was done in, until the middle 1800s, when the Fire of 1846 gutted the town, and combined with the Civil War and the period's economic developments to end the bubble, Nantucket prospered and the Captains built their Georgian, Federal and Greek Revival mansions, leaving some four hundred houses here that are more than a hundred years old.

Nantucket's present economy depends largely on tourism, but commercial fishing is still a significant activity. In a unique way Nantucket depends on the past to attract people here, and depends on the present to keep them coming. The Island's exotic whaling history captures the imagination, but its sun, sand, flora and moors bring one sharply into the present.

Reach Nantucket by ferry from Woods Hole (three hours, cars allowed) or Hyannis (two hours). We urge you not to take a car there. You will have a time finding a place to put it, and the entire Island is exuberantly and easily reached by bicycle. (Bring your own or rent one here.)

Nantucket doesn't allow camping out or sleeping in vehicles.

Public beaches are Jetties Beach, Surfside, Cisco, 'Sconset, Dionis and Madaket.

See you on the road!

1. Cape Cod Canal—Sandwich

Number of miles: 17
Approximate pedalling time: 2 hours, 15 minutes
Terrain: Flat
Surface: Good
Things to see: The Canal, Sandwich Glass Museum, Sandwich
Town Hall, Dexter Grist Mill, Hoxie House, Heritage
Plantation, Shawmee Pond, Shawmee Crowell State Park

This lovely and varied ride starts at the Cape Cod Canal, just under the Bourne Bridge. There is a parking lot here, and restrooms (during the summer season only) maintained by the U.S. Army Corps of Engineers.

Leave your motorized bike-carrier here, mount up and turn right onto the paved access road which runs along the Canal. This road is for government vehicles (a rare sight) and bicycles only.

Follow the contour of the Canal, which, in the warm months, is full of boats, large and small. The current is swift, six-seven knots at times, and often the sailboats seem to be standing still. Near the end of the Canal you'll come to the enormous NEPCO electrical power generating plant. Skirt right around it on the Canal side, and arrive at the Sandwich-Cape Cod Canal Marina. Go to the parking lot, turn left through it, and continue bearing left, past the large Coast Guard Station and the fish company where fresh fish is unloaded and prepared for shipment. Just past here is a gate which you go around, continuing to the very end of the Canal where there is a small beach. When we rode there (in the late fall) the moon was rising over Cape Cod Bay, the navigation lights were flashing, and we could see the buoys marking the entrance to the Canal. A beautiful sight!

Turn around and come back along the roadway to Coast Guard Rd. Turn left, past the Coast Guard Station on your right. At the stop sign turn right onto Town Neck Rd. Just over the railroad tracks come to a "T" with Tupper Rd. Turn left onto Tupper. Stay on Tupper past Rte. 6A, to the tiny center of Sandwich.

In this small area there are many places of interest to see.

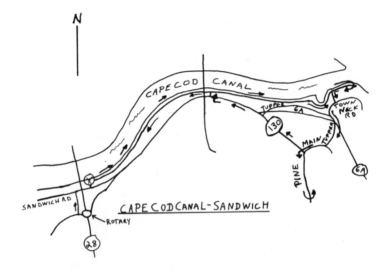

CAPE COD CANAL-SANDWICH

How to get there: Cross the Bourne Bridge. At the rotary turn right then right again, downhill to the road going under the bridge. Turn right then left to the parking lot at the Canal.

Turn left onto Rte. 130, on the left is the Sandwich Glass Museum; just across the street, on Shawmee Pond, is the Dexter Grist Mill; and up Rte. 130 a bit on the right, on the shore of the pond, is the Hoxie House. The Thornton W. Burgess Museum is also here, at 4 Water St. Burgess wrote the Peter Rabbit stories here—over 170 books and 15,000 daily columns!

The Dexter Grist Mill was built around 1650 and still grinds cornmeal which can be purchased here. The mill is open from mid-June through September.

The Hoxie House, a classic saltbox, was built in 1637, which would make it the oldest house on Cape Cod. It was acquired by the town and beautifully restored. It is also open from mid-June to September. Shawmee Pond is a jewel of a pond, teeming with wild geese, ducks, and swans in season. It is an artificial lake created around 1633 by the settlers who built a dam to provide water power for the mill. In April the fish ladder is packed with thousands of leaping herring (alewives) coming upstream to spawn.

After you have enjoyed all of these goodies (and if you have some time and a few dollars left), turn around and head north on 130. In about a mile you come to Pine St. Turn left and go uphill for 0.6 mile until you come to Heritage Plantation. This is a large place, dedicated to antique America. It consists of beautiful gardens, a working windmill, a 1912 Carousel, a round Shaker barn, antique automobiles, etc. It is open from 10:00 a.m. to 4:00 p.m. from May 1 to mid-October.

When you are ready to leave, return (downhill this time) to Rte. 130. Turn left on 130, past an old sprawling cemetery on the right, past Shawmee-Crowell State Park (one of two on Cape Cod with campsites—first come, first served!). When you arrive at the junction with 6A go left onto it, but you have to turn right and then left to do so. At the fork of Rte. 6A and 6, bear right where the sign says ROUTE 6 AND SAGAMORE VILLAGE. Pass through Sagamore Village and you'll soon find yourself at the Rte. 6 bridge over the Canal. The route parallels the Canal here. Turn right at the bridge and go directly to the access road alongside the Canal. Turn left onto it and retrace the bike route the three and a half miles back to your starting place at the Bourne Bridge.

2.   Bourne

Number of miles: 18.5
Approximate pedalling time: 2 hours, 15 minutes
Terrain: Varied, long flat stretches, some hills
Surface: Good
Things to see: Cape Cod Canal, Cataumet Methodist Church,
Aptuxet Trading Post and Windmill, communities of Bourne,
Monument Beach, Pocasset, Cataumet and Megansett (North
Falmouth)

The ride begins in the parking lot on the east side of the Canal
under the Bourne Bridge. There are picnic tables and restrooms
here. These facilities as well as the Canal and its "Tow Path" are
maintained by the Army Corps of Engineers. Mount up and go left
on the Canal Service Road heading south. This is a hard-packed
gravel road. After a mile, at the site of the railroad bridge, you'll
reach the end of this leg. Walk your bike down the embankment
and over the tracks to the parking lot. Ride through the lot and
alongside the Canal on Jefferson St. to the Point; here, you're
almost at the south end of the Canal.

Now retrace the route to the parking lot, turn right on Bell
Rd. and ride out to Shore Rd. Turn right on Shore Rd. Bear left at
the fork where there is a small traffic island. Pass Old Dam Rd. on
the left. At a sign which points to POCASSET-2 MILES, Shore Rd.
appears to "T"; in fact, it jogs right and then left in front of the
railroad station. There's a Cumberland Farms store here. Continue
on Shore Rd. You're now in the community of Monument Beach.
Upon reaching the Pocasset River, stop at the bridge and take a
look at the boats. This is a colorful, picturesque scene. There's a
tiny harbor, but evidently the draft is deep because there are some
enormous boats moored here. This area is called Pocasset.

Continue on Shore Rd. past Barlow's Landing. Just before
going under an overpass, you'll see a sign to Cataumet's Marina on
your right. Ride in for a look at the boats and beautiful Red Brook
Harbor. Then go under the underpass and up the hill—which is
the first real hill we've encountered on this ride.

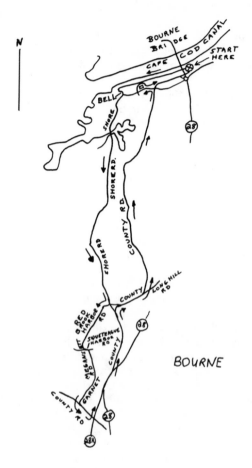

How to get there: Cross the Bourne Bridge. At the rotary turn right, then right again, downhill to the road going under the bridge. Turn right, then left to the parking lot at the Canal.

Take a hairpin right on Red Brook Harbor Rd. From the top of the hill you can see what used to be a windmill and is now a private house. Ride downhill to Parker's Boat Yard, also located on Red Brook Harbor. This community is called Cataumet. There are numerous side roads leading to the water which you may want to explore. On this stretch you'll also see the cranberry bogs for which the Cape is justly famous. When you cross Scraggy Neck Rd., Red Brook Harbor Rd. becomes Squeteague Harbor Rd. At the intersection with Meganset Rd. turn right going slightly downhill on Meganset. Here, Meganset Rd. becomes Garnet Rd., and you have just crossed into North Falmouth.

When you come to County Rd., turn left. Cross the railroad tracks. Shortly, County Rd. will "T" into Rte. 28A where there is a sign saying CATAUMET. Turn left onto 28A. You'll go up a long grade and then bear off to your left again onto another branch of County Rd. where there is a sign to BARNSTABLE COUNTY HOSPITAL and CATAUMET. This starts as a gently rolling road but it becomes a fairly steep uphill as it takes you past a drive-in where you could pick up some fried clams or fish and chips before going on.

Continue on County Rd. at its intersection with Shore Rd. Soon you'll see the Cataumet Methodist Church and cemetery. The building dates from 1765. At the fork with Long Hill Rd., bear left, staying on County Rd. In two more miles, after a couple of significant uphill grades, you'll reach a six-way intersection where there will be signs to PROVIDENCE—BOSTON—MONUMENT BEACH. Turn left on Shore Rd. You'll be able to see the Aptuxet Windmill and Trading Post from Shore Rd. Turn right onto Aptuxet Rd. and head for the windmill. Just beyond it is the Aptuxet Trading Post, originally built in 1627. There is a modest charge for the tour, which is offered from April to October 31.

After your visit, return to the intersection and take Sandwich Rd. back to the Bourne Bridge and your car.

3. West Barnstable—Sandy Neck

Number of miles: 10.3
Approximate pedalling time: 1 hour
Terrain: Varied
Surface: Good
Things to see: Old Village Store, West Parish Meeting House, Sandy Neck, Great Marshes

Turn right on Meetinghouse Way (149) to start your ride. You'll promptly pass the Old Village Store. We bought excellent cheese here for a roadside snack and enjoyed poking around the store. Go uphill. At the crest you'll get a view across the Great Marshes. There is a sidewalk along this two-lane country road which you may use. In about a mile, you'll come to a fork with a road going off at 45° to your right. It is just before a large sign saying "6 WEST—BUZZARD'S BAY—BOSTON EXIT AHEAD. Turn right before the sign, going past the West Parish Meetinghouse on your left. You are on Cedar St. Pass Willow St., Gemini Dr. and Cedarcrest La. The next is Maple St., 0.7 mile from the Meetinghouse; turn right. This is a gently rolling country road. Cross the railroad tracks and turn left on 6A.

Your route parallels the Great Marshes here. This extensive marsh comprises 3,000 acres. The early settlers used the "salt hay" collected here for such varied purposes as fodder, bedding, compost, thatching, and insulation. If you're ever wondering what all those little wooden boxes are that dot such areas, your curiosity can now be satisfied; they are bird houses for tree swallows attracted to the marsh to eat the insects, and wooden traps for horse flies (see Paul and Ruth Sadlier, SHORT WALKS ON CAPE COD AND THE VINEYARD, THE GLOBE PEQUOT PRESS).

Proceed on 6A to the fork with High St. Bear left up High St. and enjoy another view of the Great Marshes. When you come to Howland Lane, turn right and rejoin 6A turning left. In short order, turn right on Sandy Neck Rd. Ride past marshes and sand dunes to the parking lot. From there go swimming, and hiking and birding on the marked trails winding through the six miles of

How to get there: Travel east on 6A between Sandwich and Barnstable. In West Barnstable watch for a traffic light at the junction of Rte. 6A and Meetinghouse Way (Rte. 149). Turn right onto 149. Cross the railroad tracks and park on the right.

Sandy Neck dunes. The beach, being on the bayside of the Cape, is a pebbly one, but nevertheless beautiful and inviting. This site is formally called Scortin Neck Beach and Nature Recreation Area. After your visit return to 6A on Sandy Neck Rd. Turn left and proceed on 6A until you come to Meetinghouse Way. Turn right and return to your car in the railroad parking lot.

4. Barnstable—Cummaquid

Number of miles: 10.8
Approximate pedalling time: 1 hour
Terrain: Gently rolling
Surface: Good
Things to see: Colonial Court House, Sturgis Library, Trayser
   Memorial Museum

Come out of the Library parking lot and head east on 6A (also called Cranberry Highway). You'll soon pass the Barnstable Comedy Club, which is an amateur theater, and the Barnstable County Court House. This building, completed in 1774, houses exhibits of flags and paintings. A film depicting Cape Cod's history is presented. Visitors are welcome on weekday afternoons from 1:30 to 4:30. 6A is very busy here and very narrow. There is a sidewalk on the left and we recommend its use where there are no pedestrians.

About two miles from the start of the ride you'll pass the post office in the tiny community of Cummaquid. Turn left on Keveney Lane and head toward Mill Creek and Hallets' Mill Pond, going downhill. When you cross the bridge you enter a corner of Yarmouthport, and Keveney Lane becomes Mill Lane. The view of the marsh and the impressive Anthony's Cummaquid Inn is absorbing. Water St. goes off to the left shortly after crossing the bridge. Continue on Mill Lane. Return to 6A and turn right heading back to Barnstable.

If you have time, when you get to Rte. 6 on Mill La., turn left and ride a half mile to Yarmouthport to the intersection with Strawberry La. on the right and Church St. on the left. Along this stretch are several attractions to visit briefly or to linger over. Three notable houses, which represent three hundred years of New England architecture, are open to the public: the Colonel John Thatcher House (1680), the Winslow Crocker House (1780), and the Captain Bangs Hallet House (1840). They are open to the public. The Botanical Trail commences at the Hallet House. The houses and trail are administered lovingly by the Historical Society of Old Yarmouthport.

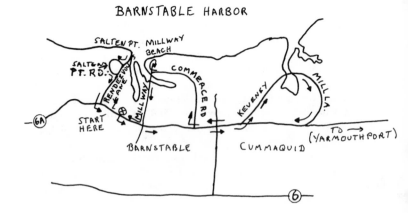

How to get there: Take 6A to Barnstable and watch for the Sturgis Library on your left shortly after passing Rendezvous Rd. Park in the library's parking lot.

After enjoying Yarmouthport turn around and head west again on Rte. 6A. Turn right on Commerce Rd., which circles a marsh and crosses Maraspin Creek. At Mill Way, turn right for a short ride to the parking lot at Blish Point overlooking Mill Way Beach and Barnstable Harbor—dotted with islands—sheltered by Sandy Neck across the way (which you may visit on the West Barnstable ride).

Retrace the route up Mill Way past the town docks to 6A. Turn right. Ride past the Sturgis Library (where your car is parked) then turn right on Rendezvous Lane for another short jaunt to the water. On the way down to, or back from, the end of Rendezvous Lane (which dead ends at the water, providing a good picnic site), turn into Salten Point Rd. This road makes a loop and returns you to Rendezvous Lane. It offers some stunning glimpses of the harbor, as well as a closer look at the life style of some of Barnstable's burghers whose well appointed houses and lawns are on display around this circle. Return to 6A, turn left and head back to Sturgis Library. Built in 1644, the library's holdings include a Bible printed in 1603, as well as material relating to Cape Cod's history and genealogy.

The Trayser Memorial Museum is also located in Barnstable on 6A. It was originally a Customs House. An old jail building is on the grounds. The collection is open to the public for a modest charge Tuesday through Saturday afternoons from 1:00 to 5:00.

5. Woods Hole—Falmouth

Number of miles: 26.5
Approximate pedalling time: 3 hours
Terrain: Varied—a lot of flat areas, other definitely hilly areas
Surface: Good
Things to see: Woods Hole Oceanographic Center, Woods Hole
    Aquarium, views of Buzzard's Bay and Vineyard Sound,
    Falmouth Historical Society Museum, Nobska Point
    Lighthouse

Ride south on 28A and bear right onto Palmer Ave. at the flashing caution light. Go down Palmer to the bottom of the hill and turn right at the fork onto a very pretty, narrow country road called Sippewisset Rd. Turn right on Beccles Rd. for a brief loop which returns you to Sippewisset Rd. When you get to the crest of the hill, you'll see the enormous Cape Codder Hotel on the bluff.

Upon leaving the crest, you'll be riding mainly downhill to Woods Hole. At the first stop sign, your route becomes Quisset Ave. When you come to Quisset Harbor Rd. turn right and go down to look at the beautiful Quisset Harbor. Come back up to the stop sign and turn right on Quisset Ave. This downhill run will bring you abruptly into the center of Woods Hole on what is now called School St. Eel Pond is the crowded anchorage to your right as you come into town; the buildings bordering the pond are those of the three marine research institutions: the National Marine Fisheries Service, the Marine Biological Laboratory, and the Woods Hole Oceanographic Institute. Watch for the research vessels R/V "ALBATROSS" and R/V "DOLPHIN," and visit the Woods Hole Aquarium, which is run by the National Marine Fisheries Service and is free. Quisset Ave.—now School St.—"Ts" into Water St. Go right on Water St. to the research facilities and to see the Candle House. A unique ship's bow sticks out of the front of the building.

To continue your route, take a loop to Nobska Point and back by heading east uphill (away from downtown Woods Hole) on Water St. past the ferry landing, and past the cove, turning right

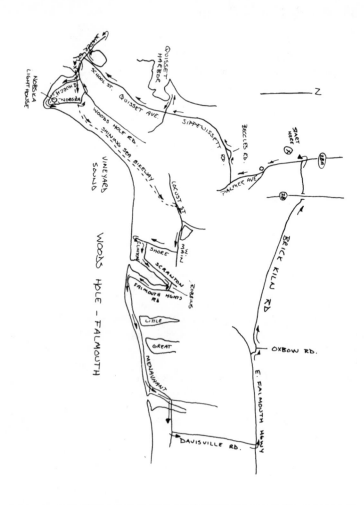

How to get there: Head south from the Bourne Bridge on Rte 28A to West Falmouth. Park south of the intersection of Rte. 28A and Brick Kiln Rd. in the parking lot of a tiny shopping center.

on Church St. From the Point, the view of Vineyard Sound and the shoreline is superb. Enjoy picnicking and swimming at the point. Now bear on around the point on what is now Nobska Rd. Ride under the Bicycle Trail and then turn immediately left and go sharply uphill on Woods Hole Rd. Continue bearing left and return to town. Head for the Woods Hole Steamship Authority parking lot. Turn at the sign ALL CARS FOR BOATS TURN HERE. Cross in front of the Steamship Authority and enter the parking lot through the pedestrian entrance. Ride through the parking lot and go under the underpass.

You are now on the three and one-third mile long Shining Sea Bikeway connecting Woods Hole and downtown Falmouth, paralleling Fay Rd. along Vineyard Sound.

You'll emerge from the dramatic bikeway onto Locust St. Bear right. At the fork bear right again onto W. Main St. by the Falmouth green. Watch for the elegant 1790 colonial across the green, which is the Falmouth Historical Society Museum.

At Shore St. turn right and go down to the water, see the Town Beach, then go back up Shore two blocks to Clinton and turn right. Ride about five blocks to Scranton Ave. on the Falmouth Inner Harbor. Skirt this beautiful active harbor by going left on Scranton, right on Robbins Rd. at the top of the harbor and right on Falmouth Heights Rd. to go down the east side. This is another site from which you can ferry to Martha's Vineyard.

Bear right at the fork onto Grand Ave. and turn sharply left as it skirts Vineyard Sound. Continue along this road, which becomes Menauhant Rd., passing Little Pond and Great Pond. At the fork with Ocean Ave. (or Vineyard St. as it may be named), turn left and go inland staying on Menauhant Rd. At its intersection with Emerson (on the left), bear right staying on Menauhant. Cross Acapesket Rd. then cross the bridge over Green Pond then turn left on Davisville Rd.

Turn left on East Falmouth Highway. In about three quarters of a mile, cross the Coonamesett River and turn right on OxBow Rd. Curve around uphill and turn right going uphill on Brick Kiln Rd. Follow Brick Kiln to Rte. 28. Go under Rte. 28 to Rte. 28A and turn left to return to the shopping center parking lot.

6. Osterville—Centerville

Number of miles: 14
Approximate pedalling time: 1½ hours
Terrain: Hilly
Surface: Good
Things to see: Towns of Osterville and Centerville, East, West and Great Bays, Crosby Ship Yard

Begin this ride in the village of Osterville. Park on Main St., at the intersection of Main, Parker Rd. and Bay St. Mount up and do a loop around this lovely village by riding downhill on Main St. (following the sign to HYANNIS). When you get to the A&P take a right uphill onto West Bay Rd. Turn right again on Wianno Ave. going past the post office and the library. Return to Main St.

After the loop, you're back on top of the hill. Now bear left in front of the Osterville Baptist Church, then go right following the sign which reads FALMOUTH—17 MILES. At the fire station, turn right on Pond Rd. You may use the sidewalk along Pond Rd. Turn right on Bumps River Rd. You'll encounter some uphills along here and then a nice downhill to a pond. At the first fork, bear right remaining on Bumps River Rd. At the "T" intersection turn left on what is Park Ave., though it may not be so marked, and ride the short distance to Main St. where you turn right. Now you're in for a treat, as Centerville's Main St. is exceptional. There are stately old houses on both sides of the street, a handsome church, and the 1865 Country Store which is full of handmade crafts and gadgets to nourish your curiosity and pleasure.

When Main St. intersects with S. Main St. there's a traffic light. Turn right following the sign to OSTERVILLE. Proceed on S. Main St. Now enjoy the views of East Bay. Turn left onto East Bay Rd. following it to the "T" intersection with Wianno Ave. Turn left onto Wianno (may not be marked) and ride to Dowses Beach. Wianno Ave. "Ts" into Seaview Ave. Turn right and follow Sea View to its end. After passing the gatehouses, backyards, and driveways of the rich, and after experiencing an occasional open-mouthed stare at a house which would be more comfortable on a

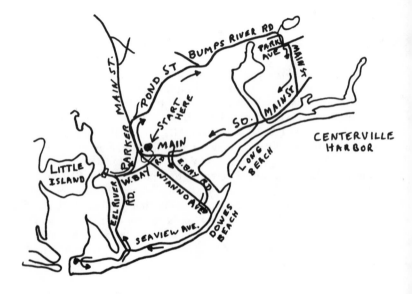

OSTERVILLE - CENTERVILLE

How to get there: From the intersection of Rtes. 149 and 28, head east toward Hyannis on Rte. 28. Take South County Rd. to the right. It becomes Main St. and delivers you to the center of Osterville.

back lot at Warner Brothers than here facing the restless oceans and inlets of the Cape, you'll arrive at the end of Sea View Ave. Here you'll be overlooking a bar called Dead Neck, Grand Island and West Bay.

After enjoying the scene, retrace your route to just past Eel River and turn left on Eel River Rd. It will "T" into West Bay Rd. Turn left. Immediately you'll be at the Crosby Boatyard. Operational since 1840, this yard was the home of the Crosby Cat, the original Catboat. The Crosby Boatyard still handcrafts pleasure boats and provides marina services to boaters.

Leaving Crosby's, turn left on West Bay Rd., then turn left on Parker Rd.—which turns into Main St.—and return to the village of Osterville.

7. The Cape Code Rail Trail

Number of miles: 19.6
Approximate pedalling time: 2½ hours
Terrain: Flat to moderately hilly
Surface: Excellent
Things to see: Fresh water lakes (called ponds), forests, salt and
   fresh water marshes, cranberry bogs, Rock Harbor and all
   the flora and fauna contained therein

This ride, except for a few places where roadways intersect, is
completely free of all motor vehicle traffic; close to twenty miles of
eight-foot-wide paved bike path! As of this writing, December
1983, it runs along the abandoned right-of-way of the Penn Central Railroad from Rte. 134 in South Dennis to Locust Rd. in
Eastham (¼ mile from the Salt Pond Visitors' Center), passing
through the towns of Harwich, Brewster, and Orleans. The original
railroad was built in the early 1880s and finally abandoned for
railroading purposes in 1965. The Massachusetts Department of
Environmental Management has plans to extend the trail for three
miles to the Eastham-Wellfleet town lines.

Since there are parking lots at each end of the trail as well as at
Rte. 124 in Harwich and Nickerson State Park in Brewster, you
could begin your ride at any one of these points. Rest areas and
comfort stations can be found at the Dennis Town Hall just west of
the Rte. 134 terminus, on Old Bass River Rd., Nickerson State
Park, the Salt Pond Visitors' Center, and at most town beaches.

If you decide to start at the Rte. 134 end, as you travel along
the trail you will pass many fresh water ponds, created thousands
of years ago by tremendous blocks of ice left behind by the retreating glacier. Sand Pond, Hinkley's Pond, Seymour and Long Pond
are a few of these "kettle" ponds you will pass. At the intersection
with Rte. 6A in Brewster you will come alongside Nickerson State
Park, 1750 acres, with four ponds ranging in size from 18 to 204
acres, over 400 camp sites and eight miles of bike paths. Just past
the park the trail will go under Rte. 6A through its own small
tunnel and enter the area of salt marshes such as the NAMSKA-

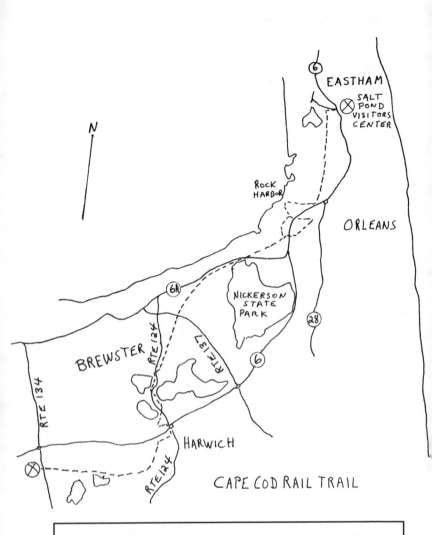

How to get there: For the West end (Rte. 134), take Rte. 6 to Rte. 134 and go south to the entrance to the trail. For the East end, (Eastham), take Rte. 6 to the Salt Pond Visitor's Center in Eastham.

KET CREEK, a classic example of a barrier beach salt marsh system which will be on your left. After this when the trail reaches Orleans it will take a short detour down to Rockport Harbor, a small fishing harbor with a beach for swimming. Farther north the fresh water ponds reappear and the ride ends at Locust Rd. in Eastham, a quarter mile from the Salt Pond Visitors' Center on Rte. 6. This beautiful facility of the Cape Cod National Seashore blends artistically into the landscape and through its exhibits and films provides a fascinating glimpse into the human and natural history of the Cape—plus giving you a breathtaking view of a tremendous salt pond.

8. West Yarmouth—South Yarmouth

Number of miles: 14.5
Approximate pedalling time: 2 hours
Terrain: Moderately hilly
Surface: Good
Things to see: Aqua Circus, Judah Baker Windmill, Yarmouth Herring Run

Start this ride by parking your car in the parking lot of the Home Federal Savings Bank on the southeast corner of Rte. 28 (Main St.) and Berry Ave. Proceed across 28 and go north on Higgins Crowell Rd. A sign will point to ROUTE 6. Go through the typical Cape Cod pine forest here, uphill for eight-tenths of a mile to the juncture with Buck Island Rd.; turn right. This is a well paved, two lane road which goes by cranberry bogs, off to the right. Come to West Yarmouth Rd. Turn left on this two lane road. Pass through patches of open countryside, still climbing, as you go inland from the shore. Three miles into the ride you come to Old Town House Rd.; turn right. There is a country feeling out here, where the land is sparsely settled. Old Town House Rd. is a big three lane road still going uphill. In one and a quarter miles turn right on Station Ave., a gently rolling road, which goes mostly downhill.

Just past the Regional High School on your left, across the football field, turn right onto Long Pond Dr. Skirt Long Pond, which you can glimpse through the trees to your left. At the end of Long Pond, after passing Winslow Gray Rd. on the right, turn left on Mercury Drive. At the point where Venus Rd. comes in from the right and Mars Lane also goes off at an angle to the right, continue straight ahead on Mercury Dr., which will "T" into Lyman Lane. Turn right on little Lyman Lane and go down to Rte. 28, turn left and then immediately right onto Wood Lane. Go past a small, wooded lane divider where there's a statue of a fireman. Just past this spot, turn right onto Wood Rd., a narrow residential street. Cross Main St. (Rte. 28) and the road you're on is now called River St., which takes you down to and briefly along the Bass River.

WEST YARMOUTH – SOUTH YARMOUTH

How to get there: From the west take U.S. 6 to Rte. 132, 132 South to 28, and 28 East to West Yarmouth, to Berry Ave. The Yarmouth Police Station is on the northwest corner.

At the fork with Pleasant St., bear right on River St. Soon after the fork, you will come to the Judah Baker Windmill on the bank of Bass River in tiny Windmill Park. There's a nice little beach here. The Windmill was originally built in 1791 in South Dennis and moved here in 1863. The town now owns it and is restoring it. Continue on River St., which swings around 90° to the right and then comes to South St. where there's a stop sign. Turn left onto South St. which takes you down to Shore Side Dr. Run Pond is on your right. Smuggler's or Bass River Beach is here on the curve just as you get to the shore line. There are lots of motels, cottages, and quiet houses. You are now on Shore Side Drive. Proceed along the waterfront. There are houses between you and the water but you can go down any one of the streets running off to your left to the shore. There are several public beaches along this road.

At the stop sign with Seaview Ave., turn left past the Beach House Motor Lodge to the point, a nice place to take a break and get a great, unimpeded view of the ocean. Turn around and go straight up Seaview Ave. to Main St., on Rte. 28. There's a stop sign. Turn left. The Aqua Circus is on the right. They have six shows a day, featuring dolphins. Stop and take a look. Just past the Aqua Circus comes South Sea Ave. and a traffic light where you turn left and return to the shore line.

Sea Gull Rd. comes up in a mile, turn left onto it, and head for Sea Gull Beach. Lewis Pond will be in sight to your left. Stretches of the road become a causeway across the marshes. Beautiful Sea Gull Beach is open from 8:00 a.m. to 10:00 p.m. There are restroom facilities. After your swim and/or picnic, return to South Sea Ave. via Sea Gull Rd. Turn right on South Sea and then, about four blocks up, turn left onto Silver Leaf Lane, which will take you five-eighths of a mile to Berry Ave. There is a stop sign but no street sign; however, you'll be able to identify it because Silver Leaf Lane jogs to the left after it crosses Berry. Turn right on Berry, which will take you back up to S. Main St. where you started your ride.

9. West Dennis—Harwichport

Number of miles: 18
Approximate pedalling time: 2 hours
Terrain: Flat to moderately hilly
Surface: Good
Things to see: Towns of Harwich and Harwichport, Cape Cod
    Rail Trail, Allen Harbor, Glendon Beach, Swan River, West
    Dennis Beach

Start this ride in the parking lot of the Ezra H. Baker Public School on the corner of Rte. 28 and Trotting Park Rd.

Head north on Trotting Park Rd. A stop sign comes up shortly at the intersection with Centre St. There is a little triangular shaped park here and the substantial Congregational Church of South Dennis can be seen on the right after crossing over Centre St. Continue north on what is now old Main St. There are many handsome houses out this way. About one mile from the church there is a fork where there is a little stone marker in a tiny park. Main St. goes to the left. Continue on Main, past Duck Pond Rd. for about a quarter of a mile to the next intersection with High Bank or Great Western Rd. (Liberty Hall is on the corner.) Turn right and go the short distance to Rte. 134 where there is a traffic light. Turn left and ride about a quarter of a mile to the point where the Cape Cod Rail Trail begins. As of the fall of 1983, this bike path ran for 19.5 miles from Rte. 134 all the way to the National Seashore Visitors' Center in Eastham. You now have a 4½ mile, traffic free ride all the way to Rte. 124. When you reach 124, turn off the trail and ride down Rte. 124 approximately one mile to Main St. in Harwich. Turn left on Main.

Riding along on Main St. watch for Bank St. as you enjoy Harwich, which is a picturesque village with old houses and a pleasant air.

Leaving Harwich on Bank St. there is a good downhill run to Harwichport past cranberry bogs here and there, for a nice one and a half mile ride. At the junction of Rte. 28 and Bank St. turn right and ride west on 28 until the fork where Rte. 28 goes off to

41

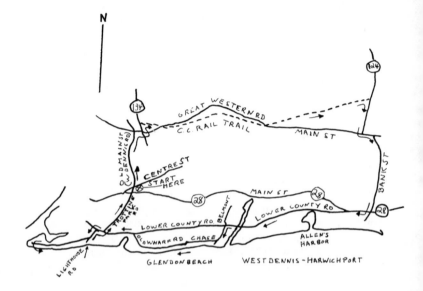

How to get there: From the west take Rte. 6 to Rte. 134 in South Dennis. Take 134 south to Rte. 28, turn right onto Rte. 28 and proceed three-eighths of a mile to the intersection of Rte. 28 and Trotting Park Rd.

the right and Lower County Rd. bears left. (If you have time, take a detour down to Wychmere Harbor by turning left when Bank St. "Ts" into Rte. 28 and going east for about a quarter of a mile to Wychmere Rd. Turn right. Enjoy your visit to this scenic harbor, then return to Rte. 28, head west, and continue the bike trail.) You take Lower County Rd.

Ride through Harwichport with its interesting old houses, churches and little shops. Continue past Allen's Harbor, a tiny protected harbor right off the road, and over the Herring River into Dennisport where you'll see some of the southernmost part of that town. There is a lovely view of the harbor, the docks, and the windmill out on the point. This is a nice place to stop.

Turn left on Belmont Rd. and at the end of it turn right on Chase Ave. where the road parallels Motel Mecca. Follow closely when it goes right and then turn immediately left onto Old Wharf Rd. At the five-way intersection, cross Sea St. and continue straight ahead on Old Wharf Rd. and you'll come upon Glendon Beach, which is public. Old Wharf Rd. ends at the stop sign at Lower County Rd.; turn left.

Shortly afterward cross over the Swan River with its fascinating marsh lands. Turn left onto Lighthouse Rd. There will be a sign to the Town Beach right across from a marsh; continue down to the extensive and beautiful West Dennis Public Beach.

When you're ready to go, return up Lighthouse Rd. to Lower County Rd. and turn right. Ride as far as Trotting Park Rd.; turn left. Ride the one mile back to your starting place at Rte. 28 and Trotting Park Rd.

10. Harwich—West Chatham

Number of miles: 14
Approximate pedalling time: 2 hours
Terrain: Rolling hills
Surface: Good
Things to see: Town of Harwich, Brooks Free Library, Town
Beach, Cockle Cove, Ridgevale Beach, central Cape Cod
countryside

Start your ride in the center of Harwich, on Main St., near the
juncture of Rtes. 39 and 124.

Harwich is a lovely, small, New England town with its graceful
white Congregational Church. It has some five antique shops on its
Main St. Great for browsing. If you have pannier bags you might
find that small gee-gaw you've looked for everywhere.

Ride east on Main St., past the Brooks Free Library. You might
stop in here to see the collection of 19th century statuary by John
Roger. They are set in a Victorian atmosphere. Then you pass the
bandstand and ball field, to a "Y" where you will bear right on
Chatham Rd. Main St. is lined with trees that are larger and taller
than those found closer to the sea. One and a half miles down
Chatham Rd., you'll come to a "T" intersection with Rte. 28. Turn
right on 28 and ride a short distance to Deep Hole Rd.; turn left
and ride a half mile down to the small but lovely town beach.
There are restrooms here. When you're ready to leave, take the
road that starts just across from the restrooms. This is Uncle Venies
Rd. although it may not be so marked.

Ride up one quarter mile and turn right onto S. Chatham Rd.
The route is parallel to the beach and ocean here, and provides a
fine view across the salt marsh. Pass Soundview coming in from the
left. Once you pass over into Chatham this road becomes Deep
Hole Rd., although there might not be a sign. Go uphill for a short
distance, then the road levels off just before the "T" intersection
with Pleasant St. There's a stop sign here. Turn left onto Pleasant
St. and ride up to Rte. 28. Turn right onto 28. There's a village
store and snack bar on the corner. This is a rolling road. Follow it

How to get there: From the west take Rte. 6 to Rte. 124 in the township of Harwich. Go right on 124 to the center of Harwich.

for three quarters of a mile, past Rte. 137 which comes in from the left, to Cockle Cove Rd. There's a sign saying COCKLE COVE; turn right and go down to the cove and Ridgevale Beach.

After visiting the beach, retrace the route back up the same road to Rte. 28, where you turn right and then left on Sam Ryders Rd. It's mostly uphill here for almost one mile to a "T" intersection with Queen Anne Rd. Turn left here. Stay on Queen Anne Rd. for four miles now, to the intersection with Rte. 124. Note that Queen Anne Rd. is not well marked so follow the map and instructions carefully. Pass Church St. and then cross Rte. 137 which bends here and is called Morton Rd. on your left and Long Pond on your right. Continue straight and soon Cemetery Rd. will come in from your right and merge into Queen Anne Rd. Stay on Queen Anne. You'll come to a stop sign on Rte. 39 which you cross over and continue past a small pond, then Bucks Pond and Josephs Pond, all on your left. Just past the ponds, the road widens. At the intersection of Queen Anne Rd. and Rte. 124, there is a stop sign. Turn left onto Rte. 124, which is called Pleasant Lake Rd. From here the route is mostly downhill for one mile to Harwich, and your starting place.

11. West Brewster—Dennis

Number of miles: 21
Approximate pedalling time: 3 hours
Terrain: Hilly
Surface: Good to excellent
Things to see: Stony Brook Grist Mill, Chapin Memorial Beach,
New England Fire and History Museum, Sesuit Neck Harbor,
Sealand, The Drummer Boy Museum, Museum of Natural
History and Smock Windmill, Josiah Dennis Manse

Begin this ride on Rte. 6A just west of Rte. 137 (Long Pond Rd.).
Park in the lot of the New England Fire and History Museum.
Come out of the parking lot and turn right onto Main St. (Rte. 6A).
At the fork where 6A goes right, take the left hand, which is Stony
Brook Rd. There's also a sign indicating a Bike Route in this
direction. You'll pass Smith Pond on the left and then a series of
ponds.

You'll soon begin a stiff uphill and then take a steep downhill.
About three quarters of a mile from the fork you'll come upon the
Stony Brook Mill on the left. This grist mill still works to show you
how it was done. It is open from 2:00-5:00 p.m. Wednesdays,
Fridays, and Saturdays in July and August.

There's a fork just beyond the mill; here, bear left onto Setucket Rd. This road is hilly. You pass a lovely placid little pond and
go through a forested area. Two miles from the fork of Setucket
and Stony Brook Rds. there is another pond where you bear right,
remaining on Setucket Rd. There is much open, unsettled country
through here, very much like parts of Connecticut. In another mile
cross Rte. 134, then cross River Rd. Setucket becomes a roller
coaster, winding around and rolling up and down. You'll be able to
see Follins Pond to the left from the ridge. At the crest of a hill, at
the intersection of Setucket, North Dennis, and South Yarmouth
Rds. turn right onto South Yarmouth Rd. South Yarmouth may not
be marked so look for No. Dennis Rd. coming in from the left at
this point. Here there are some downhill runs as you head back to
Rte. 6A, just about a mile away. Arriving at 6A, turn right and go
three-fourths of a mile to New Boston Rd. on the left. Take a

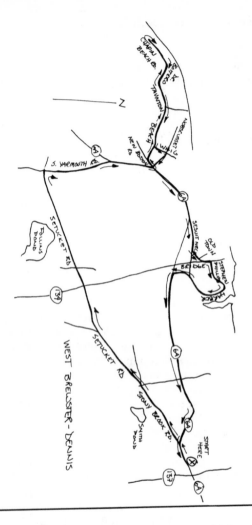

How to get there: From the west take Rte. 6A just into Brewster and watch for the New England Fire and History Museum on the left, just before the Town Hall. From the east take 6A through Brewster past the intersection of Rtes. 124 and 137 to the Museum.

hairpin turn to the left onto New Boston Rd., which is just across from the Dennis Public Market. Almost immediately there is a fork with Beach St.; bear right onto Beach. Easy Bay View comes in from the right; go left heading for Chapin Beach on Taunton Ave. It's a three way fork; take the one farthest left. Taunton soon turns into Dr. Bottero Rd. This is a dune and grass area with water on both sides, now called Chapin Beach Rd. at the George Halliday Chapin Memorial Beach. Continue out through the dunes—great for sunbathing, getting lost in, or what have you. Follow the paved road as far as it goes and you come to Chapin Beach. Return the same way, via Dr. Bottero Rd., Taunton Ave., and Beach St. Stay on Beach as far as Whig St. on the left. It's the next street after Tory La., of course. Turn left onto Whig St. Go to the next intersection which is with Nobscusset Rd. and turn right. At this corner is the Josiah Dennis Manse, a grey shingled house, built in 1736 for the Rev. Dennis (manse means the residence of a minister).

Follow Nobscusset Rd. back to Rte. 6A, then turn left and head east toward East Dennis and Brewster. Ride along 6A, using the sidewalk wherever possible, for slightly more than a mile to the fork where Sesuit Neck Rd. bears left. Ride along on it for one-half mile until Old Town La. comes in from the left at a fork with a little traffic island. "T" into Bridge St. shortly and turn left and then right onto Stephen Phillips Rd. and follow it as it turns left, down to the seashore and right on Harbor Rd. to Sesuit Neck Harbor. Continue around the busy little harbor on Harbor Rd. until it becomes Sesuit Neck Rd. Follow this to the intersection with Bridge St., where you turn left and go up to 6A. Turn left onto 6A and ride past the salt marshes into Brewster. There are several attractions along this section of the bike route. Sealand of Cape Cod is an extensive commercial aquarium. The Drummer Boy Museum is also a commercial venture. The museum has thirty acres of scenic countryside and picnic grounds. If you go there, visit the restored 18th century Smock Windmill. The Museum of Natural History provides exhibits illustrating Cape Cod's ecology, a salt water aquarium, and nature trails.

At the intersection where Stony Brook Rd. goes off to the right, go left. This road is now Main St. in Brewster as well as being Rte. 6A so you'll soon come to the start of the ride at the New England Fire History Museum.

12. Brewster—Nickerson State Park

Number of miles: 16
Approximate pedalling time: 2½ hours
Terrain: Moderately hilly
Surface: Good
Things to see: Nickerson State Forest, Brewster, Brewster and
    Harwich countryside

Start this ride in Nickerson State Park just off Rte. 6A in Brewster.
In the summertime the parking lot just inside the entrance to the
park is a holding area for campers. After Labor Day you can park
here but in the summer, park either in the parking lot located
1000 feet west of the entrance, off Rte. 6A, or go into the park, a
short distance straight ahead just past the ampitheatre to where
there is a parking area on your right.

You can begin the ride here and start off on the bike path to
the right. This paved path is just for you and it winds its way mostly
downhill for approximately two miles through the park.

Just after you pass the dumping station and the fire tower (off
to your left), stay on the bike path as it turns 90° right at an
intersection of the park road (which turns left) and three other
roads, all of which are outside the park. Access to these by car is
barred by a gate. There are several private homes here on Wind-
swept Rd. and Joe Longs Rd. Here the bike path parallels Joe
Longs Rd. In a quarter of a mile leave the park bike path and cross
over to Joe Longs Rd. just before it "Ts" into Milestone Rd., then
turn left onto Milestone Rd. Ride on Milestone for about one and a
half miles until it "Ts" into Rte. 137, which is also called Long
Pond Rd. Turn left and ride two and a half miles through a forest
where the colors are gorgeous in the fall, to the point, just before
Rte. 6, where Long Pond Rd. goes 90° right. Turn right and ride
through scrub pine forests on either side. There will be an occasional glimpse of Long Pond on the right. When Long Pond "Ts"
into Rte. 124, turn right and get on the Cape Cod Rail Trail which
runs along Rte. 124 here. Take this marvelous bike path north for
approximately 5½ miles as it criss-crosses Rte. 124 by Long Pond

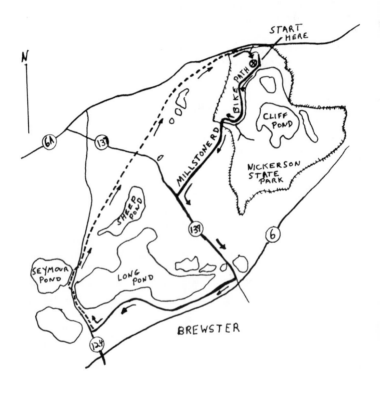

N

START HERE

BIKE PATH

CLIFF POND

NICKERSON STATE PARK

MILLSTONE RD

6A

13

137

6

SHEEP POND

SEYMOUR POND

LONG POND

BREWSTER

124

How to get there: Take Rte. 6A east to Brewster and the entrance to Nickerson State Forest. Coming down 6A from the east, you'll find the State Forest on your left about one and a half miles west of the junction of Rtes. 6 and 6A.

and Seymour Pond, then off to the north through the woods, past the Brewster Golf Club, right up to where it borders the waiting areas in Nickerson State Park. Here you turn right at the small sign "Nickerson State Park" and ride the very short distance on this spur of the Cape Cod Rail Trail into the park and return to your starting place. Just after this point, the Rail Trail goes left and under Rte. 6A, so if you find yourself doing that, you have gone too far.

13. Chatham

Number of miles: 21.5
Approximate pedalling time: 3 hours
Terrain: Hilly to flat
Surface: Good
Things to see: The beautiful town and harbors of Chatham,
  Chatham Fish Pier, Chatham Lighthouse

Begin the ride in the parking lot of the shopping center at the junction of Queen Anne Rd. and Rte. 28 in Chatham. It's a five point intersection. When you leave the parking lot bearing right on Queen Anne Rd., you'll be on a marked Bike Route. Pass the First Church of Christ, Scientist on the left. At the "Y" continue right on Pond St. (Queen Anne Rd. goes up to the left). Circle enormous Oyster Pond, which has a public beach. At the stop sign of the "T" intersection, turn right onto Stage Harbor Rd. At the "Y" intersection with Cedar St. turn right onto Cedar St. When Cedar St. "Ts" into Battlefield Rd., turn left and ride along Battlefield until the "T" with Champlain Rd. Turn left onto Champlain, still following the Bike Route. Very soon Champlain makes a 90° bend to the left at the shore of Stage Harbor. You can see Stage Harbor Lighthouse out there as your route takes you along the shore of this beautiful harbor. Look for the nun and can buoys marking the channel. There are fishing boats at Old Mill Boatyard and Chatham Fisheries affording an interesting scene.

Champlain Rd. turns left and becomes Stage Harbor Rd. Bear left and shortly you will come to a stop sign where Bridge St. is on the right; turn right onto it. There's a nice little dock here. Go over the drawbridge and go straight until you come to a "T" with Morris Island Rd. Turn right to go down Morris Island Rd. On the left is the Chatham Lighthouse. When you come to Little Beach Rd. straight ahead, you bear right, continuing on Morris Island Rd. Bear left and down and across the causeway. You're on Morris Island and when you come to the end of the road there's a sign saying QUITNESSET. At this point the Monomoy National Wildlife Refuge walking trail starts, so take an exploring walk. When you're ready, double back across the dike. Stage Harbor is on the

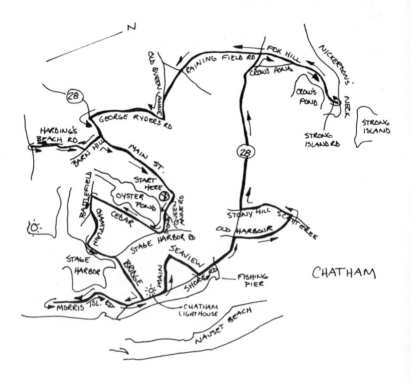

How to get there: From the west take Rte. 28 directly into Chatham and proceed to the starting place in the center of Chatham.

left. At the stop sign continue straight past the Chatham Lighthouse.

Take in the view, looking past Nauset Beach to the Atlantic Ocean. In a few blocks at Main St. turn left and go up past all the little shops—very picturesque—to the corner of Seaview and Main; turn right and go up a steep curve to the right which takes you to Shore Rd. Turn left. Ride one long block, then turn sharply right at the sign TOWN OF CHATHAM FISH PIER. From this pier fishing boats go out all year round to supply us with fresh haddock, cod, and scallops.

Go back to Shore Rd. and turn right. At the traffic light Old Harbor Rd. crosses Shore. Turn right onto it and go downhill here. At the "T" of Old Harbor and Scatteree Rds., turn left on Scatteree, again following the Bike Route. Bend around to the left, downhill past Old Mail Rd., on what is now called Stony Hill Rd. until you come to Řte. 28; turn right. It's downhill here. At a "Y" with Crow's Pond Rd., continue bearing left until you come to Fox Hill Rd. Turn right and follow Fox Hill Rd. up and out on Nickerson's Neck to the end of the public road. Take Strong Island Rd. to the left and go to the end, where it overlooks Strong Island. Across on the left is the mainland of Cape Cod. This whole area is protected by the long arm of Nauset Beach. Back track to Fox Hill then bear right and return with a view of Crow's Pond on the left as you ride. At the intersection of Crow's Pond and Fox Hill Rds. bear right on Fox Hill. At the stop sign intersection with Rte. 28, continue straight across on what is now called Training Field Rd. Cross Old Comers Rd. and soon come to Old Queen Anne Rd. which comes in from the right. Training Field Rd. merges with it. Continue, bearing to the left, on Old Queen Anne Rd.

When George Ryders Rd. comes in from the right, turn right onto it and follow it past the airport to Rte. 28 where you turn left and very shortly come to Barn Hill Rd. Turn right. This road goes downhill and curves left and right to a "Y" with Hardings Beach Rd. Turn right on Hardings Beach Rd. and follow it to the beach. This is a public beach with sand dunes. It extends for a mile to the left to Stage Harbor Lighthouse.

After spending some time at this beach, re-trace the route back to Rte. 28 where you turn right and head back into another two lane road, and your starting place.

14. Orleans

Number of miles: 13.2
Approximate pedalling time: 2 hours
Terrain: Moderately hilly
Surface: Good
Things to see: French Cable Museum, Town Cove, Nauset
Harbor, Nauset Beach, Packet Landing, Rock Harbor

Start your ride in the Stop and Shop parking lot, which is just across from the Orleans Inn of the Yankee Fisherman on Rtes. 6A and 28, just before the Orleans-Eastham town line.

Leave your bike carrier here and ride out to 6A and 28; turn right. You quickly come to a "Y" intersection where 28 and 6A split. Bear left on Rte. 28. In one third of a mile come to Cove Rd.; turn left and go down the short hill to the shores of Town Cove. The tiny Orleans Yacht Club is located here at the innermost end of this long cove which is bordered by Orleans and Eastham. Come back up the short but steep hill. You will be turning left here, but first take a look into the French Cable Museum on the corner. The building housed the United States terminus of the original Atlantic Cable and is now a museum, open only Friday through Monday, 2:00-4:00 p.m. It is full of fascinating old equipment.

Now turn left onto 28 and almost immediately 45° left at a "Y" to Main St. where you turn 90° left, on your way to Nauset Beach. Another short ride brings you to the intersection of Main St. and Tonset Rd. Turn left onto Tonset. Over on your left there is a nice view of Town Cove. Continue on Tonset past woods on the left and characteristic Cape Cod houses on the right, past Gibson Rd. and Brick Hill Rd., straight out to the dead end where Tonset Rd. overlooks Nauset Harbor, which is a cut through Nauset Beach. This is three and a half miles from your starting point.

Turn around and go back up Tonset Rd. to Brick Hill Rd.; turn left. There should be a sign here directing you to Nauset Beach. Continue on Brick Hill as it twists and turns, passing Champlain and Hopkins La., passing through some wooded areas which are alive with color in the fall. About one and a half miles from your

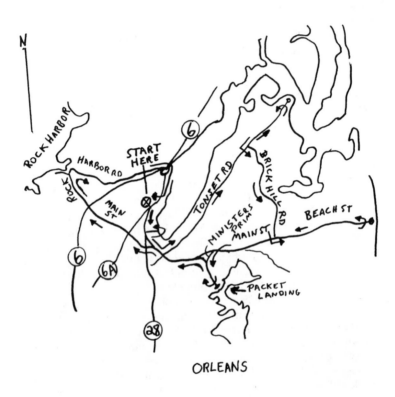

N

ROCK HARBOR

HARBOR RD

START HERE

ROCK

6

TONSET RD

BRICK HILL RD

MAIN ST

MINISTERS PRIM MAIN ST

BEACH ST

6

6A

PACKET LANDING

28

ORLEANS

How to get there: From the south take 28 or 6A into Orleans and proceed to the Orleans Inn of the Yankee Fisherman just before the town line of Orleans and Eastham. Turn left into the shopping center parking lot.

turn onto Brick Hill, there is a "T" intersection with Beach Rd. There may not be a road sign here, but turn left and you'll see the "1810 House" on the left, just after the intersection.

In six-tenths of a mile, over to your right is a stunning view of the salt marshes with the beach in the distance. You are close to the beach at this point. From here to the beach is downhill now. At the beach there's a large parking lot, dressing rooms, telephone, a little refreshment stand plus one gorgeous beach where you can swim, picnic, and/or walk in the dunes.

Come back up the hill, retracing your route. Pass the intersection with Brick Hill Rd. and continue straight on Beach Rd., passing the Raleigh Neck Inn and then, at a "Y" intersection with Main, bear to the right onto Main St. Just before getting to Meeting House Rd. on the right, turn left onto Ministers Prim, a short, oddly named dirt road, which immediately blends into River Rd., and proceed the short distance to Packet Landing, so named from the time, long ago, when packet boats came here from New York and New Jersey on a regular schedule.

Retrace your way back and, at the "Y," bear left, rejoining Main St. where you again turn left. You'll pass the Orleans Arena Theatre and then come to the stop light at the intersection of Main and Tonset. Continue on Main St., crossing Rte. 28 and then 6A. You are passing through the Orleans business district here, with shops of all kinds as you head toward the bay side and Rock Harbor. The road goes gently downhill and in about one and a half miles you arrive at Rock Harbor. This is a tiny, bustling little harbor, chock full of fishing boats—both for professional fishermen and for amateurs who can charter here. It's a very business-like place with a restaurant and convenient dockside parking lot.

Next, take Rock Harbor Rd. around to the left (a left hand turn, facing inland), and you will soon find yourself paralleling Rte. 6. Just past the Eastham-Orleans town line turn right at the rotary, continuing around it to where a sign says 6A and 28 RIGHT, ORLEANS 1 MILE. Turn right. From here you can see the Orleans Inn of the Yankee Fisherman just up ahead and your starting place.

15. Eastham—Coast Guard Beach

Number of miles: 9.7
Approximate pedalling time: 1½ hours
Terrain: Moderately hilly
Surface: Good
Things to see: Salt Pond Visitors' Center, Eastham Historical
    Society Museum, Eastham Windmill, Great Pond, Nauset
    Light Beach, Coast Guard Beach

Start the ride in the parking lot of the Salt Pond Visitors' Center
where you can leave your "motorized" vehicle, if you have one.
There are two of these Visitors' Centers in the National Park
Service's Cape Cod National Seashore and both are beautifully
designed and integrated architecturally into the landscape. They
not only provide you with fascinating information about the human and natural history of the surrounding area through exhibits
and illustrated orientation programs, but situated as they are on
high ground, they afford marvelous vistas of the seashore.

The Salt Pond Visitors' Center overlooks the quite amazing
and beautiful landscape of an enormous salt pond. Plan to spend at
least several hours at the Center upon your return. Be sure to
explore a bit of the Braille Nature Trail before you leave the
parking lot. Proceed toward Rte. 6, past the Eastham Historical
Society Museum on the right. It's open Wednesday and Friday
afternoons in July and August.

At Rte. 6 take a left and proceed, using the sidewalk, a short
distance to Depot Rd. just across from the Town Hall; turn right.
Depot Rd. forms a triangle with, and joins Jemima Pond Rd. Stop
and take a look at the Eastham Windmill, which is in the triangle.
It still works! Proceed down Jemima Pond Rd. past Long Pond on
the right to Great Pond Rd., turn right.

If you'd like to take a short side trip to the Cape Cod Bay side,
continue straight ahead to First Encounter Beach. Return to Great
Pond Rd. and proceed past the Town Landing and public beach on
the shore of Great Pond. If you'd like a swim in the warmer waters
of a lake, try this one.

N ——

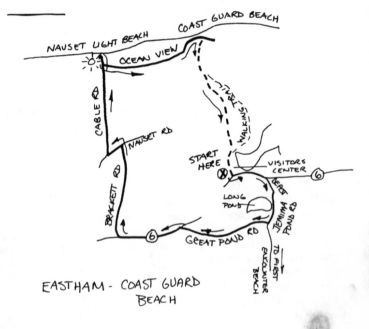

EASTHAM - COAST GUARD
BEACH

How to get there: Take Rte. 6 from the north or south
into Eastham. Watch for the sign SALT POND
VISITORS' CENTER.

Go uphill from Great Pond, continuing on Great Pond Rd. through a residential part of Eastham, back to Rte. 6, about one mile from the turn onto Great Pond from Jemima Pond Rd. When you arrive at Rte. 6, turn left but use the bi-walk (an extra wide sidewalk shared by pedestrians and bicyclists) because Rte. 6 is heavily traveled here. In three-quarters of a mile, at the stop light at Brackett Rd., there is a large green sign, NAUSET LIGHT BEACH, which is the next destination. Proceed uphill on Brackett Rd. In about one mile at the "T" intersection with Nauset Rd., turn left then immediately right onto Cable Rd. to a bluff overlooking the ocean and Nauset Light Beach. In case Nauset Rd. and Cable Rd. signs are missing, watch for the signs to Nauset Light Beach. The beach is below the bluff and the 114' high steel tower and flashing beacon of the Nauset Beach Light. The light was established in 1838. As you leave Nauset Light Beach parking lot turn left at the first intersection, which is Ocean View Dr. When Coast Guard Beach comes into sight, there is a great, sudden downhill, at the bottom of which you must yield, so watch the traffic, then whip up to your left to Coast Guard Beach. Here there is a large white building, formerly a Coast Guard Station, now an environmental education center. From the observation area at the side of the house the view is spectacular over the ocean and the tidal wetlands. If you can get back here at sunset, do so; the display of glorious colors is stunning.

After you've seen and experienced all you have time for, take the bike trail that begins just before the four car (or boat) garage. The trail crosses two spur roads and just before the first one you'll see the Doane Rock and picnic site. This lovely bike trail will take you two miles, mostly downhill, back to the Salt Pond Visitors' Center.

16. South Wellfleet—Marconi Station

Number of miles: 9.6
Approximate pedalling time: 1½ hours
Terrain: Moderately hilly
Surface: Very good
Things to see: The original Marconi Wireless Station, Marconi Beach, the Audubon Society's Wildlife Sanctuary

Leave your automobile in the parking lot of the Cape Cod National Seashore Headquarters and ride out toward the ocean and the Marconi Station site. This is very flat, almost like a plain. Then the road goes gently uphill to the top of a bluff. Here, on this bluff, Guglielmo Marconi built his wireless station and sent the first wireless telegraph message across the Atlantic to England in 1903, a message from President Teddy Roosevelt to King Edward VII. There is a display that tells the fascinating story. Lock up your bike and take a nature trail to White Cedar Swamp and Forest, crossing the swamp on a boardwalk.

Retrace your road back, past the C.C.N.S. Headquarters to the park; turn left and head toward Marconi Beach. This great beach is another of the lovingly preserved, fine white sand beaches of *your* Cape Cod National Seashore, stretching as far as the eye can see. There are bathhouse facilities which are designed low and of weathered grey board to complement, not intrude upon, the landscape. There is a boardwalk with steps leading down to the beach.

When you are ready to continue, return, pass the Headquarters again and proceed to Rte. 6. Turn left onto Rte. 6 and proceed for one and a half miles until you see the white and green sign featuring a herring gull, stating MASS. AUDUBON SOCIETY. Turn right and go straight ahead into the Society's Wellfleet Bay Wildlife Sanctuary. It's open from 8 a.m. to 8 p.m. and there is a small fee. When you reach the parking area you'll notice a pipe sticking up out of the ground which has a slot in it—and it is into this pipe that you deposit your fee!

There are picnic tables, rest rooms, and a bike road. Try to plan your day so that you have ample time to explore the nature trail on

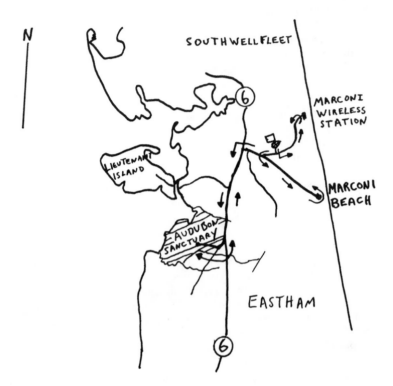

N

SOUTH WELLFLEET

6

MARCONI
WIRELESS
STATION

LIEUTENANT
ISLAND

MARCONI
BEACH

AUDUBON
SANCTUARY

EASTHAM

6

How to get there: Proceed north on Rte. 6 to South Wellfleet. About 1¾ miles from the Eastham town line turn right after the sign "MARCONI AREA NEXT RIGHT." Proceed a half mile to the Cape Cod National Seashore Headquarters.

foot. If you go to the office, in the house to your left, you can pick up a map of the Sanctuary. The area that is particularly exciting for nature lovers is Try Island, out in the marsh. Here you can see a landscape that is particularly characteristic of the Cape and of the New England Shore—great tidal wetlands. The island permits you to go out far into the marsh and experience the space, color, smell, and rhythm of the wetlands. If you buy guides for the Sanctuary's specific walks, you will be greatly assisted in identifying the rich birdlife and flora of the marsh and woodlands. This is one of the few sites on the Cape that provides access to the wetlands.

When you leave the Sanctuary, turn left at the gate and within a few yards you'll rejoin Rte. 6. Proceed for one mile back to the C.C.N.S. Headquarters.

17. South Wellfleet—Lecount Hollow

Number of miles: 9.7
Approximate pedalling time: 1 hour
Terrain: Definitely hilly
Surface: Good
Things to see: Typical Cape pine forest, Lecount Hollow Beach,
    Ocean View Beach, White Crest Beach, bluffs

Park in the restaurant's parking lot and head south down Rte. 6 about one half mile. Just past the cemetery on your left, turn left on Cahoon Hollow Rd. Go up hill. It's short but very steep. Take the first right, which is Old County Rd. You will meander through a semi-residential area of dunes and a typical Cape pine forest. Old County Rd. is roughly parallel to Rte. 6. After about a mile and a half Bell Rd. comes in from the right. Continue straight ahead and rejoin Rte. 6. Turn left on Rte. 6 and ride about ¼ mile and turn left onto Lecount Hollow Rd. Ride straight to the ocean on this road. Lecount Hollow Beach will be at your feet. This is a lovely white beach bordered by the Cape's very special green and blue ocean. You can swim here or you may prefer to swim a little farther north of here, off Ocean View Dr. where there's a bit more privacy.

Head back down Lecount Hollow Rd. for a brief stretch to Ocean View Dr. Turn right. The crest yields a sensational view of beach, ocean, and the bluffs-dotted with summer cottages (some for rent; most private). There is a parking lot here, so ride in, lock your bike and walk down to White Crest Beach. You can wander on foot all over the bluffs; you'll see numerous trails heading off through the scrub. Continue going right on Ocean View Dr. after your swim.

When Cahoon Hollow Rd. crosses Ocean View you could detour briefly by taking a right down the steep hill to the Town Landing. If you prefer not to, continue straight for a nice long downhill giving you stunning views off to your right.

Turn left on Gross Hill Rd., which is very hilly, including a long uphill grade after the fork with Gull Pond Rd. (Depending on

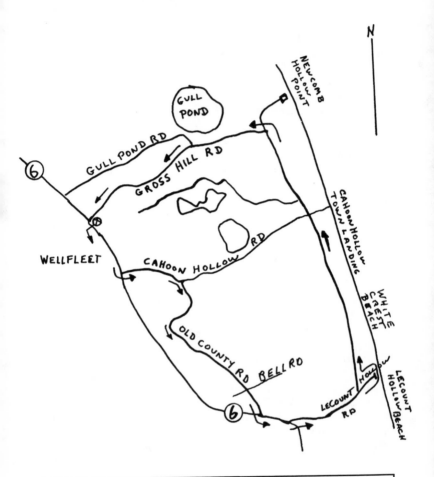

How to get there: Head toward Wellfleet on Rte. 6. Watch for the Yum Yum Tree restaurant on the southeast corner of the Rte. 6-Gross Hill Rd. intersection. There is a sign saying NEWCOMB HOLLOW-OCEAN BEACH.

the time of year, the Gross Hill Rd. road sign may be missing, taken as a souvenir, so, if you pass the turn-off onto Gross Hill you will quickly come to a dead end at Newcomb Hollow Point. Go back and take the first road to the right, which is Gross Hill Rd.) After about two miles on Gross Hill Rd. you'll return to the intersection where you left your car.

18.   Wellfleet—Great Island

Number of miles: 6.8
Approximate pedalling time: 45 minutes
Terrain: Hilly
Surface: Good
Things to see: Wellfleet, Wellfleet Harbor, Mayo Beach,
    Chequesset Neck, Great Island

Park close to the Wellfleet Post Office on the corner of West Main
St. and Holbrook Ave., then turn right (east) on West Main St.,
although you might want to visit the attractive Pisces Gallery and
Craftsman's Barn next to the post office before you start. You'll
find Wellfleet an inviting village to explore on foot as well as by
bike.

Take a hairpin turn to the right on East Commercial St. to
head down to Wellfleet Harbor. You will get a fine view of this
large, beautifully protected harbor on your way there. The town
pier at Shirttail Point warrants a stop. Ride out to the end to get
the full effect of the village, the harbor (watched over by a white,
spired church on a hill), and the dunes of Great Island, a preserve
of the Cape Cod National Seashore. At the pier you may fish or
rent a boat.

Upon leaving the pier take Kendrick Ave. west along the
shore. As in every town on the Cape here you'll pass an abundance
of guest houses and motels. Bear left at the junction with Hiller St.
and cross the Herring River. At the top of the hill, turn left into the
Cape Cod National Seashore picnic grove and parking area. Here
you will find guides to the hiking trail on Great Island. This trail is
an eight-mile round trip which you may want to do provided you
have hiking boots and good health. In any event walk some distance onto Great Island just to enjoy the ambience of this unique
natural site. Before returning to town you might want to go north
downhill on Griffin Island Rd. to the parking area. Here you can
wander along a more remote beach.

To return to town retrace your route along Chequesset Neck

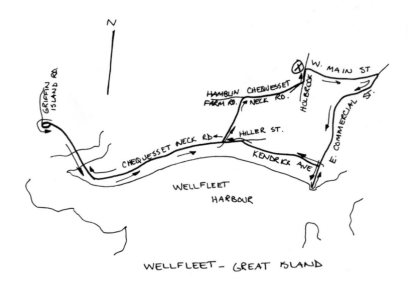

N

GRIFFIN ISLAND RD.

HAMBLIN FARM RD.

CHEQUESSET NECK RD.

HILLER ST.

CHEQUESSET NECK RD.

HOLBROOK

W. MAIN ST

E. COMMERCIAL ST.

KENDRICK AVE.

WELLFLEET HARBOUR

WELLFLEET - GREAT ISLAND

How to get there: Go toward Wellfleet on Rte. 6. Turn west at the traffic light where Rte. 6 crosses a street called Gross Hill Rd. going east and Mill Hill Rd., going west. Follow the sign to WELLFLEET CENTER.

Rd. Bear left at the "Y" staying on Chequesset Neck Rd. Chequesset Neck bears sharply right where Hamblin Farm Rd. comes in from your left. Stay on Chequesset Neck Rd. At the "T" intersection with Holbrook Rd. turn left and return to the Wellfleet Post Office on the corner of Holbrook and West Main Sts.

19. North Truro—The Highlands

Number of miles: 9.8
Approximate pedalling time: 1½ hours
Terrain: Cape Cod hills
Surface: Good
Things to see: Head of Meadow Beach, Highland Light, Highland Museum, Jenny Lind Tower, both coasts of the Cape

High Head Rd. becomes a dirt road soon after it leaves Rte. 6, at the point where it forks. Here you go left, following the sign that reads "Parking." At the end of this road is a tiny parking lot with a sign at its far end that reads "OVER SAND ROUTES—ANNUAL PERMIT REQUIRED." Hidden to the right is the entrance to the Head of the Meadow Bicycle Trail. Start the ride here and take off on your bike onto the fine, paved bikes-only trail which wanders through the sand dunes along the edge of Salt Meadow. It runs for a marvelous two miles and comes out at Head of Meadow Beach. After a visit to the beach, ride down Head of Meadow Beach Rd. toward Rte. 6. When you reach Rte. 6 turn left and then go off Rte. 6 to the right, down a short hill and then left onto Highland Rd., which passes under Rte. 6. You'll see a sign here to HIGH-LANDS—1 MILE.

Highlands means just that, so expect a long incline that levels off in a half mile, then continues up a slight grade to a "T" intersection with a sign that reads "HIGHLAND LIGHT." Turn right, go up a short hill, then turn left. You can see the Highland Lighthouse ahead of you. The Highland House Museum is on your left. Run by the Truro Historical Society, it contains everyday articles used by the Pilgrims, e.g., firearms, relics from shipwrecks, etc. It is open from 1:30 p.m. to 4:30 p.m. daily in the summer; a small admission fee is charged. Continue up to the Highland Light (also called the Cape Cod Light). It now flashes a four million candlepower beacon, warning ships, now mostly huge, heavily laden oil tankers, away from the "Graveyard of Ships."

It was originally built in 1797, then destroyed by fire and rebuilt in 1857. From the overlook you can see both sides of the

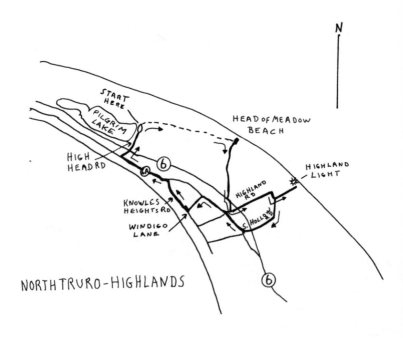

N

START HERE

PILGRIM LAKE

HEAD OF MEADOW BEACH

HIGH HEAD RD

6

A

HIGHLAND LIGHT

KNOWLES HEIGHTS RD

HIGHLAND RD

WINDIGO LANE

S. HOLLOW

NORTH TRURO - HIGHLANDS

6

How to get there: From the south take Route 6 to High Head Rd., at the eastern end of Pilgrim Lake. Depending on the season, the High Head road sign may be missing, taken as a souvenir, so watch for the sign reading, "To Rte. 6A Beach Points," with a left pointing arrow. Turn right just after that sign.

Cape, ocean and bay. As you walk to the overlook you'll see the Jenny Lind Tower—a quirky thing!—and beyond the tower the three radar domes of an Air Force Radar Station. In 1850 Jenny Lind, the "Swedish Nightingale," came to Boston for a concert. More tickets were sold than there were seats. To prevent a riot, Jenny climbed to the top of this tower, so the story goes, and sang to the crowd. In 1927 one Harry Aldrich bought the tower and moved it here.

Retrace your tracks and go downhill to the intersection where you turn left on S. Highland Rd. and run downhill. At the bottom of the grade turn right on S. Hollow Rd. This is a pleasant road, with no houses on either side, which winds its quiet way through stunted pines for a mile, until it comes to Rte. 6. Go across Rte. 6 to the "T" intersection with Rte. 6A, just a few feet from 6, and turn right. This is a pretty stiff uphill for one quarter mile, at which point the road crests and starts to roll up and down.

At approximately one and two tenths miles from your turn onto 6A you'll come to Windigo Lane on the left. Turn left onto it. You are on a bluff; wind around for a short stretch, to Cobb Rd. Turn left onto Cobb and then right where it "Ts" with Knowles Heights Rd. Stay on Knowles Heights Rd. as it wanders for a mile and a half through these dunes, along the Cape Cod Bay shore, until it rejoins 6A at the bottom of the short steep downgrade. Where 6A intersects with Rte. 6, turn left, then right where you see the sign HIGH HEAD. Go up High Head Rd. to the parking lot where you left your car.

20. Province Lands

Number of miles: 8¾
Approximate pedalling time: 1 hour
Terrain: Hilly
Surface: Excellent
Things to see: Herring Cove Beach, spectacular sand dunes, ponds, bogs, Race Point Beach, Province Lands Visitors' Center

This ride is on a specially laid out, asphalt bike path that takes you up and down some spectacular sand dunes and scrub pine forests to the Atlantic Ocean side of the tip of the Cape, then loops back through dramatically contrasting terrain.

When we rode it, in September, after Labor Day, we turned left at the first fork, just past the first underpass under Province Lands Rd., and went clockwise around the circuit. The Cape Cod National Seashore staff recommends a counter-clockwise circuit from this first fork, however. In summer, when more bikers are in blossom it is probably wiser to follow their suggestion, although the path is wide enough to pass other bicyclists. There are some great downhills with sharp curves; keep to the right and stay alert.

The area you are passing through was set aside by the "Plimouth Colony" in 1620, a remarkable act on the part of these hardy folk, preoccupied as they must have been with sheer survival.

There are several places to stop and spend some pleasurable time picnicking and/or swimming at either of the two beaches, visiting the Province Lands Visitors' Center, taking the nature walk in the Beach Forest area, or taking a bargain-priced sightseeing flight from the Provincetown Municipal Airport.

The Visitors' Center is up a steep hill from either direction and the panoramic view from its observation deck is breathtaking. There is an outdoor theater (closed after Labor Day) and inside there are movies about the area and its wildlife every hour on the hour.

The Beach Forest Trail is a one-mile loop that is well worth

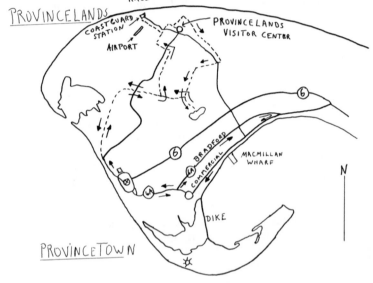

RACE POINT BEACH

PROVINCELANDS

COAST GUARD STATION

PROVINCELANDS VISITOR CENTER

AIRPORT

6

BRADFORD

COMMERCIAL

MACMILLAN WHARF

DIKE

PROVINCETOWN

N

How to get there: Take Rte. 6 out to the very end of the Cape. Go around the traffic circle to the Herring Cove Beach parking lot.

taking. Be sure you can lock your bike securely before you set out afoot. The walk is beautifully described in detail in SHORT WALKS ON CAPE CODE AND THE VINEYARD by Paul and Ruth Sadlier (Globe Pequot Press).

This is one of the nicest rides on the Cape, with short, roller-coaster hills, unique scenery, and *no* automobiles to contend with.

21. Provincetown

Number of miles: 8.5
Approximate pedalling time: 1½ hours
Terrain: Slightly hilly
Surface: Good
Things to see: The myriad wonders of Provincetown! Macmillan
Wharf, Provincetown Aquarium, Playhouse, Pilgrim
Monument and Museum, Seth Nickerson House, Herring
Cove Beach

This ride will take you on a tour of fabulous Provincetown with its
old houses, historic landmarks, fishing fleet, and artists and artisans
of all descriptions. After riding from Herring Cove Beach to the
rotary, before you enter the town proper, lock up your bike and
walk out on the dike built to protect Provincetown Harbor. The
dike, which goes over to Long Point, yields a fine view of the
harbor.

The street coming out of Provincetown to this point is one-
way, so you can't use it; instead, continue around the rotary,
retracing your route to the point where 6A heads into town. Turn
right at 6A SOUTH-PROVINCETOWN CENTER-BOSTON. This
is West Bradford St. There are two principal streets in Provincetown: Bradford St., which is two-way, and Commercial St., which
parallels the harbor and is one-way.

As you ride along Bradford, you'll pass numerous little lanes
running between Bradford and Commercial. (You will be returning along the waterfront on Commercial St.) Bradford is lined with
guest houses of all shapes, sizes, and qualities, and with little
restaurants. Pass the David Fairbanks House (1776) and the Folk
Museum. At Winslow St., three miles from the start of the ride,
turn left and ride up to the Pilgrim Monument and Museum.

As you come to the end of Bradford, you'll pass craft shops and
there will be dozens more of these on Commercial St. At the
junction with Commercial, make a hairpin turn to the right and
head back along the waterfront. At this end of town many little
cottages are jammed cheek-to-jowl along the road.

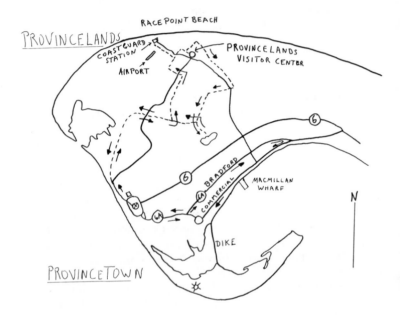

PROVINCELANDS

RACE POINT BEACH

COAST GUARD STATION

PROVINCELANDS VISITOR CENTER

AIRPORT

6

BRADFORD

COMMERCIAL

MACMILLAN WHARF

6

N

DIKE

PROVINCETOWN

How to get there: Take Rte. 6 out to the very end of the Cape. Go around the traffic circle to the Herring Cove Beach parking lot.

About a mile from the Bradford-Commercial intersection, you'll reach the downtown area. There are some older houses sprinkled through the area on the right, as well as such places as the Provincetown Art Association Gallery. Restaurants, galleries, and shops are piled on each other. Leatherwork, silverwork, antique jewelry, paintings, prints, portraits done in a single sitting—all are available here. Throngs of pedestrians make riding in this narrow street almost impossible; you'll probably find you'd rather get off your bike and push it along through the center of town—or, lock it up while you stroll here, joining the vacationers in a snack or drink at such places as the Inn at the Mews or the Café Blasé (located next to one of several bike rental stands).

Macmillan Wharf is at the five mile point on the ride. Go out on the wharf and admire the boats. If you can be here at 6:00 a.m. you can watch the commercial fishermen and their catches, and if you have two hours to spare take a cruise on one of the two grand old schooners, HINDU or OLAD. Down past the wharf there are numerous additional crafts people and portrait painters. Soon you'll pass Town Hall Square, the famous Provincetown Playhouse and Union Square with its many shops.

Turn left where Commercial St. goes almost 90° to the left at the six mile point. You'll come to the town landing and Provincetown's oldest house, built circa 1746, at #72 Commercial St. The house is open to the public. This end of Commercial St. has a number of quaint, older houses and a generally more conservative atmosphere than elsewhere, since it is a quiet residential area. A lovely inn, the Red Inn, is located here—it's open year round and serves dinner nightly.

You'll come out at the rotary at the dike after six and a half miles. Turn right and continue back toward the car. Contrary to widely held opinion, Cape Cod is not flat, but is generally rolling and includes some very steep hills and bluffs. The ride ends back at Herring Cove Beach at the parking lot.

22. Oak Bluffs—Edgartown

Number of miles: 16
Approximate pedalling time: 1 hour, 45 minutes
Terrain: Flat to moderately hilly
Surface: Fair
Things to see: Joseph Sylvia State Beach, Bike Trail, Wesleyan
    Grove Campground, State Lobster Hatchery, East Chop,
    Flying Horses, Felix Neck Wildlife Sanctuary, Ocean Park

If you begin at the junction of Bluffs Ave. and Seaview Ave., at the
landing for the Woods Hole and Nantucket ferries, proceed north
to the end of Seaview Ave. Enjoy the comings and goings of the
sailboats, fishing vessels, and ferries from Hyannis and Falmouth as
they travel in and out of Oak Bluffs Harbor.

Curve around the point on Circuit Ave. Ext. Turn right on
Bluffs Ave. Lock up your bike here and walk uphill on Circuit Ave.
(bikes are not allowed). Circuit is Oak Bluff's main street of shops,
galleries, and restaurants. Return to Bluffs Ave. At the intersection
is a carousel called with the old term "Flying Horses," which has
been a part of the Oak Bluffs scene since 1884.

Mount up again, head down Bluffs Ave. and turn left on
Central Ave. This little street will take you uphill to Wesleyan
Grove Campground. At the top of the hill bear left then right on
Montgomery Ave. to come out at Trinity Park Tabernacle. Turn
right and circle around the park. Explore this unique community
of narrow streets crowded with ornate, colorful, tiny cottages. At
this site, Baptist and Methodist Camp meetings have been held
since 1835. Tenting gave way to cottages in the middle 1800s.
After making the circuit, turn right onto Highland Ave. at the foot
of Tabernacle Park, and then right again on Siloam Ave. Siloam
joins Dukes County Ave. Bear right and proceed to Lake Ave.
Sunset Lake is on the left with Lakeside Park on its west side.

Turn left on Lake Ave. which borders Oak Bluffs Harbor and
then right on Commercial Ave., which may not be marked. It goes

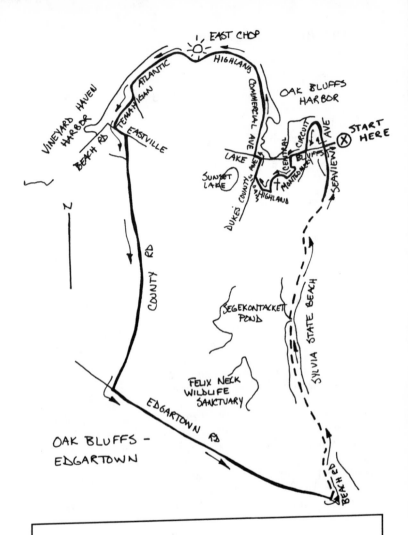

How to get there: In Oak Bluffs: Go to the end of Bluffs Ave. to the ferry landing. From Edgartown: Leave town on Main St. (Vineyard Haven Rd.); ride to the intersection with Beach Rd. and start the ride at the south end of the Bike Trail, which parallels Beach Rd.

alongside the water and then up a short hill. Go up onto the bluff and around the point of land called East Chop on Highland Dr. and Atlantic Ave. You'll pass the East Chop Lighthouse and then enjoy a downhill which yields a view of Cape Cod, Vineyard Haven Harbor, West Chop, and the West Chop Lighthouse. Your road goes sharply left soon after this and then you turn right on Temahigan Ave.

When Temahigan "Ts" into Eastville Ave. turn left. The Martha's Vineyard Hospital marks the spot. Eastville may not be marked. (Note: This is the junction to Vineyard Haven. If you want to go there, turn right, then left onto Beach St. to cross the causeway. Go over a little drawbridge. Stop at the turnout to take in the activity in Vineyard Haven Harbor on the right and Lagoon Pond on the left.)

Ride east on Eastville Ave. to County Rd. Turn right and head south. In a little less than half a mile you may turn right following the sign to the State Lobster Hatchery. This research facility and hatchery is open to the public.

At the "T" intersection with Edgartown Rd. turn left and head southeast. There are many private roads here which are closed to cars but which bicycles may use if you want to do some exploration.

In about a mile and a half from the turn onto Edgartown Rd., turn left into the Felix Neck Wildlife Sanctuary, a 200-acre tract abutting Segekontacket Pond and comprising marked nature trails.

When you leave Felix Neck, turn left onto Edgartown Rd. In about two miles you'll come to an intersection where Beach Rd. joins Edgartown Rd. from the left. There is a sign reading BIKE RTE. CROSSING. Turn sharply left and north here to start the Bike Trail to Oak Bluffs. The Trail parallels Beach Rd. for the six-mile trip. There is a sign pointing to OAK BLUFFS STATE BEACH. The Bike Trail is paved. Stay on the right! It is not one-way. You'll soon see Segekontacket Pond on your left and the beach for Edgartown residents on your right. Sylvia (Oak Bluffs) State Beach is a two-mile-long beach located on this barrier. Stop anywhere for swimming, fishing, and picnicking.

Upon leaving the beach, continue north toward Oak Bluffs.

About two and a half miles from the State Beach the Bike Trail ends. Continue up the bluffs on Seaview Ave.

Complete the ride at Ocean Park with its octagonal bandstand and border of gingerbread houses. On summer Sundays a band plays concerts here.

23. Chappaquiddick

Number of miles: 7.5
Approximate pedalling time: 1 hour
Terrain: Flat to rolling
Surface: Fair
Things to see: East Beach, Cape Poge Light, Wasque Wildlife
 Preservation Area, Dike Bridge, ON TIME ferry

Get on the tiny ON TIME ferry from Edgartown to Chappaquiddick which plies its brief route continually from 7:30 a.m. until midnight during the season (and until 6:00 p.m. in the off-season). People are charged 25¢ and a bike and rider 75¢ for the trip. It's the greatest transportation bargain around. The passage takes only a *minute,* so savor every *second* of the view of Edgartown, with its elegant captains' houses and lighthouse, and of Edgartown Harbor, dotted with boats of all kinds. To your right is Katama Bay. Debark onto Chappaquiddick and proceed straight ahead; there will be many bicycles and they are instructed to KEEP RIGHT. RIDE SINGLE FILE. You'll go by a beach club on the left and Caleb's Inlet on the right. The route goes up an incline. Be sure to pause at the top for the view of Edgartown and its environs. At about the two-mile point, Chappaquiddick Rd. curves sharply 90° right. Straight ahead is an unpaved dirt/sand road. This is Dike Road. Take it and it will lead you to the famous Dike Bridge (now a part of American history), East Beach, and Cape Poge. East Beach, about three miles from the ferry landing, is part of the Cape Poge Wildlife Preserve and is a beautiful white sand beach on the Atlantic. A long neck, Cape Poge, extends to the north. Trek out there for privacy, dunes exploration, and to see the Lighthouse and views of Martha's Vineyard. This sand bar protects Cape Poge Bay, as it curves around in an elbow shape. Camping on these beaches is not allowed, but you can spend day after day out here experiencing the sun and the sand (and the mystery of the Chappaquiddick Dike Bridge). When you leave the beach, retrace your route up the dirt road, past the two houses and the Toms Neck Farm Preserve on the right, which is a commercial shooting range.

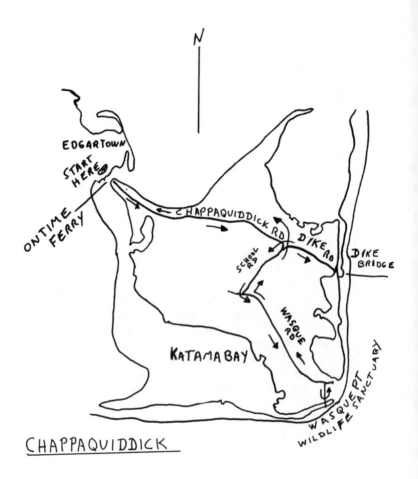

N

EDGARTOWN

START HERE

ON TIME FERRY

CHAPPAQUIDDICK RD

DIKE RD

SCHOOL RD

DIKE BRIDGE

WASQUE RD

KATAMA BAY

WASQUE PT WILDLIFE SANCTUARY

CHAPPAQUIDDICK

How to get there: Go to the wharf at the end of Main St. in Edgartown, park and ride to the Town Dock which is at the foot of Daggett St.

When you come to paved Chappaquiddick Rd. again, turn left. Here the road is also called School Rd. Take it to a "T" intersection with Wasque Rd. on the left (paved) and Litchfield Rd. on the right (unpaved). Turn left onto Wasque Rd. It soon becomes a dirt/sand road so you have to ride carefully. Like many roads on Martha's Vineyard, Wasque Rd. has many private roads leading from it. Continue to Wasque Pt. where the one hundred and fifty acre Wasque Reservation is open to the public. When you come to a fork and one way signs, take the road that goes 90° right to the beach. Return to the School Rd. junction after exploring Wasque Pt. and turn right and ride back to the ON TIME ferry.

24. Edgartown—Katama (South) Beach

Number of miles: 10.5
Approximate pedalling time: 1¼ hours
Terrain: Flat to moderately hilly
Surface: Fair
Things to see: Numerous Captains' houses, Thomas Cooke House Museum, First Federated Church, Edgartown Lighthouse, ON TIME ferry, Felix Neck Wildlife Sanctuary, Sheriff's Meadow, Katama (South) Beach

This ride tours Edgartown and then loops down to Katama Beach and back. It starts at the Town Dock in Edgartown. Go along Dock St. the brief distance between Main and Daggett to the ON TIME ferry landing and the Public Wharf. Go up to the observation deck of the wharf for views of Edgartown, the harbor, and Chappaquiddick Island, then ride up Daggett St. to North Water St. (If Daggett is one way you can walk your bike this short distance.) To your right is the Daggett House Inn built in 1750 and open to the public. Turn right. From here to the end of the street are Martha's Vineyard's handsomest Captains' houses. Several were built at an angle to afford views of homebound ships rounding Cape Poge. The chimneys, picket fences, door fans, and other well-crafted wood details contribute to the elegance of these houses, built in the early 19th Century. The bike route takes you past some but not all of these, so do some additional touring of stately Edgartown if you have time.

At the end of N. Water St., lock up your bike and walk to the Lighthouse, then turn left onto Starbuck Neck Rd. Starbuck Neck Rd. "Ts" into Fuller St. Turn left here and head back toward Main St.

At Morse St. turn right and then immediately left on N. Summer St. On this street pass the little red brick St. Andrew's Church, the Christine Pease House, and the Captain Henry Holt House (1828), now a guest house.

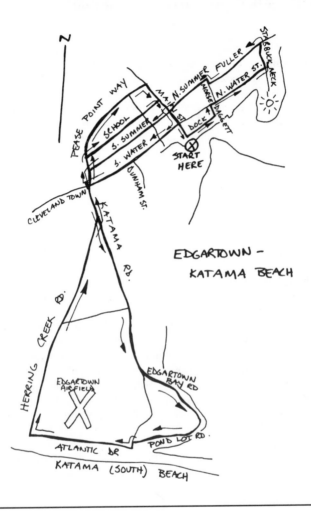

How to get there: Take the Edgartown Rd. from Vineyard Haven or Oak Bluffs or the West Tisbury Rd. from the direction of Gay Head. Take Main St. to the Town Dock.

On Main St. turn left, go one block, and then right on S. Water St. Here you'll pass several old, handsome white frame houses with bright green shutters, all of them of historic interest. These houses form the complex of the Harborside Inn. Proceed on S. Water St. You'll soon see Dunham St. going off to your left; go down Dunham to explore that area if you like; otherwise, proceed to where S. Water meets Cleveland Town Rd. and Katama Rd. and turn right. Go uphill to School St. and turn right. On the corner of School and Cooke Sts., visit the Thomas Cooke House Museum, then ride back to Main St. (Edgartown's one way streets require lacing back and forth in this manner.)

At Main St. turn right in front of the Courthouse. At S. Summer St. turn right again. Enjoy the diversity of the shops on Main St. and S. Summer St. S. Summer St. has many historically significant buildings, including the First Federated Church (1828) as impressive inside as out, with its box pews, chandeliers, and organ case.

When you return to Pease Pt. Way, turn left and head south to Katama Beach, on Katama Rd. Take the bike path on the left side of Katama Rd. Bear left at the fork with Edgartown Bay Rd. At the fork with Town Lot Rd., remain on Edgartown Bay Rd. Circle around the point. The road's name changes to Pond Lot Rd. The barrier beach can be seen from here. Proceed west to rejoin Katama Rd. Turn left heading toward Katama Beach. Your road "Ts" into Atlantic Drive which parallels Mattakesset Herring Creek. Katama Beach is a beautiful three-mile-long white sand beach. There is surf on the ocean side of the barrier and salt water pond swimming on the bay side.

When you're ready to leave the area, go west. You'll notice only a few scattered vacation houses and sense a feeling of open space unusual for Martha's Vineyard. Turn right on Herring Creek Rd., ride past the air field and Crocker Rd., and rejoin Katama Rd.

When you cross S. Water St. the road becomes Pease Pt. Way once more. Take it to Main St. At the junction with Main St. you may turn right, going past the Dr. Daniel Fisher House and the Methodist Church, to end your ride at the Town Dock at the foot of Main St.; or, if you would enjoy a side trip to a nature sanctuary, cross Main St. and continue north. Here, Pease Pt. Way is called

Planting Field Way, and it will take you directly to Sheriff's Meadow. This eighteen-acre wildlife preserve has foot trails through woods and marshlands, including a six-mile loop around Eel Pond with Vineyard Sound as a backdrop. After your visit retrace your route to Main St. and turn left to reach the Town Dock.

25. Vineyard Haven—Lambert's Cove

Number of miles: 15.5
Approximate pedalling time: 2 hours
Terrain: Hilly
Surface: Good
Things to see: Vineyard Haven, West Chop, Lambert's Cove Rd.,
    Seamen's Bethel, Williams Street houses, Cedar Tree Neck

Start this ride at the ferry landing in Vineyard Haven. If you had to bring your car, park it in the town parking lot across from the Steamship Authority lot. Since the island is small and parking is scarce, it would be better to leave your car at Woods Hole and just bring yourself and your bike.

Facing away from the dock, turn left on Water St. and then right on Beach St., then go uphill the short distance to Main where you turn right. Main St. now goes uphill toward West Chop. As you climb, you can take in all of beautiful Vineyard Haven Harbor. The hill soon crests and you start a downhill run of nearly a half mile. At the bottom of the hill, Main St. changes its name to West Chop Ave.

As you go out on the West Chop bluffs the houses get larger. One mile farther on West Chop Ave., which rolls up and down, you'll notice a BIKE ROUTE sign on the left side of the road. At the top of West Chop you are overlooking the ocean and your road goes to the left around the flagpole. The Bike Route, which you follow, goes around the point in a loop. At the point where Franklin St. comes in from the right, you continue straight ahead, following the BIKE ROUTE sign. Within a short distance you will have completed the loop and are back at West Chop Ave. where you turn right.

Come back on West Chop Ave. to Woodlawn Ave., the next street after the Public Library. You must turn right here because Main is one-way at this point. From Woodlawn turn left on Franklin St. Ride to Spring St. and turn left. Go one block and turn right on Williams. When you come to the "T" intersection with Pine

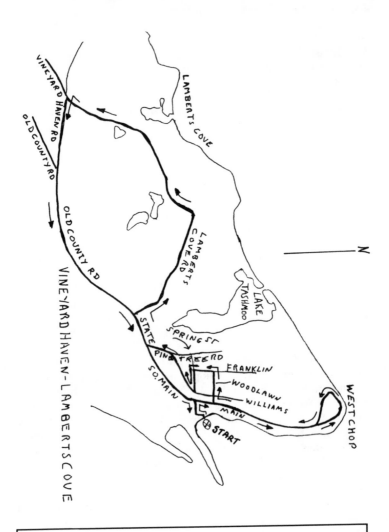

How to get there: Take the ferry from Woods Hole to Vineyard Haven. If you take one of the ferries to Oak Bluffs, follow the signs to Vineyard Haven.

Tree Rd. turn left. Pine St. then "Ts" into State Rd. at an angle where you turn right, heading west, downhill on curving, rolling State Rd.

In six-tenths of a mile you come to a turnout on the right with a magnificent view of Lake Tashmoo and the Elizabeth Islands over rolling hills. In less than a half mile you should see a sign for LAMBERT'S COVE. Turn right at the sign, onto Lambert's Cove Rd. If the sign is missing there should at least be a sign on the left side reading: GAYHEAD 17   VINEYARD HAVEN 2. You're now in horse country, with old farms and stone walls and a patch of forest now and again. One mile from the turn onto Lambert's Cove Rd., start a nice downhill run. Just before this hill is the entrance to Cranberry Acres, one of three privately owned camp grounds open to the public.

In a half mile you pass into West Tisbury and go abruptly uphill, then around a curve and down again. This is a hilly road but very scenic with views of forests and open, flat areas on either side. Pass Duarte Pond on the left and then an old country cemetery on the right. In another four-tenths of a mile, start a brief but steep uphill climb to beautiful little Lambert's Cove Methodist Church. Lambert's Cove Rd. curves around to the left, past Seth's Pond and up a four-tenths of a mile long grade to the intersection with Vineyard Haven Rd. Take a sharp left turn onto Vineyard Haven Rd. heading back toward Vineyard Haven.

If you are someone who loves to walk along nature trails, you can take a side trip at this intersection by turning right onto Indian Hill Rd. Follow it for three-quarters of a mile to the end. Just before the turnaround, a sign on the right directs you to Vineyard Sound. Take this dirt road one mile to the Cedar Tree Neck Wildlife Sanctuary, a three-hundred-acre sanctuary. No bathing or picnicking is permitted, but, clearly, communing is encouraged.

Continue the ride on Vineyard Haven Rd. Soon Old County Rd. comes in from the right and merges with Vineyard Haven Rd. Bear left and continue on this well paved road which is now taking you through flat countryside. About one and a half miles from this point pass Lambert's Cove Rd. on the left and continue on into Vineyard Haven as Old County Rd. changes to State Rd. and then to S. Main St. as it curves downward into town. Continue past Main St. to Water St. and turn left to end up where you started.

26. West Tisbury—Menemsha

Number of miles: 16
Approximate pedalling time: 2 hours
Terrain: Definitely hilly and curving
Surface: Fair
Things to see: Menemsha, village of West Tisbury, Chilmark
    Center, seascapes

Start the ride at Beetlebung Corner. Park in front of the Town of
Chilmark Town Office Building. (Beetlebung is the old Islander
name for the tupelo trees you'll see here.) Go south on South Rd.
toward West Tisbury. This first stretch of ride is level. It turns
sharply left in a few hundred yards to begin the eastward leg
toward West Tisbury. All along this portion of the ride there will
be views of ponds, hills, the ocean, and the stone walls of old sheep
farms. This is a hilly ride and, combined with the up-island's typical
narrow, curvy roads, it spells caution. In about three miles a long
downhill run offers an expansive view of moors, dunes, and ocean.
This will be followed by a gradual uphill grade before arriving in
the village of West Tisbury in about two miles. A grange, Congregational Church on the left, art gallery (with Picassoesque sculp-
tures in the garden) on the right, and fine old white frame houses
make this an attractive scene. Sir Joshua Slocum, who was the first
to circumnavigate the globe alone in his sloop Spray, made his
home here for many years before being lost at sea in 1907.

  After stopping at the West Tisbury General Store and Post
Office for an apple or a candy bar continue to the sign VINEYARD
HAVEN 7 MILES and turn left, heading north, going past the
intersection with the West Tisbury-Edgartown Rd. Soon there'll be
a sharp left—with a cemetery straight ahead for those who came to
Martha's Vineyard and never left. The terrain is fairly level along
here. Cross Mill Brook enjoying the placid Mill Pond and its ducks
and swans as you pass.

  At the fork, bear left up a slight incline on North Rd., following
the arrow to Menemsha rather than taking the right hand road to
Vineyard Haven. This lovely curving road goes through wooded

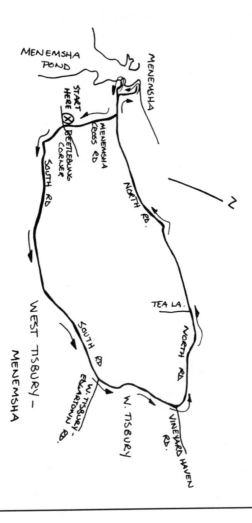

How to get there: From Vineyard Haven take County Rd. to the village of West Tisbury, then Music Rd. to Panhandle Rd. and take Middle Rd. to Beetlebung Corner.

areas of trees and thickets but also provides some views of walled pasture land and of Vineyard Sound. About three miles from the fork you will pass Tea Lane, a tree-lined narrow dirt road, to your left. This section of road continues to be quite hilly. About two miles from Tea Lane, the road crests providing a vista of Menemsha Pond. Soon you will go sharply downhill into the tiny fishing hamlet of Menemsha, past the sign to Gay Head and Chilmark. Menemsha has several docks, fishing shacks clinging to the littoral, small boats, and large fishing vessels. There are boats for charter here and a fine anchorage for visiting pleasure craft. After you go out on the dirt road alongside Menemsha Pond, come back and turn left at the first paved road and go out to Dutcher's Dock, passing a couple of art galleries, stopping for a snack and a look at the village's fish markets where everything from lobster to eels may be purchased fresh daily, and on to the public beach. After a swim or a stroll, return to North Rd., and go up the steep grade. The intersection with Menemsha Cross Rd., which may not be so marked—but should have a sign GAY HEAD—CHILMARK, is about a half mile from here; turn right onto it and return to Beetlebung Corner passing the handsome Methodist Church, the Fire Station, and Police Station.

27. Gay Head

Number of miles: 11.2
Approximate pedalling time: 1½ hours
Terrain: Definitely hilly and curving
Surface: Fair
Things to see: Gay Head Cliffs and Lighthouse, Menemsha Pond, Elizabeth Islands

Start your ride at the mile-long Gay Head Cliffs at Martha's Vineyard's westernmost tip, about 19 miles from Vineyard Haven. There are public facilities located at this National Historic Landmark, as well as snack bars and souvenir shops. These glacial cliffs, millions of years old, are made of multi-layered clays of different colors. Paleontologists have uncovered bones of ancient whales, horses, and camels in the area. One couldn't tire of the views afforded from this site: the Cliffs themselves whose clays color the water crashing into them, the western seascape of the lighthouse, the Chilmark hills, and the ponds, dunes and beaches of Martha's Vineyard.

When you leave the Cliffs bear left on the one way loop and then turn right on Moshup Trail. Head downhill toward the water. The Gay Head Town Beach is on the right. Summer houses are perched randomly among the hills and dunes, and the dunes are covered with grasses like bear's fur. Low shrubs, bushes, and stunted trees provide the vegetation at Gay Head. The effect is rather desolate but also unique and therefore arresting. Moshup Trail parallels the coast. About a mile from the cliffs Old South Rd. enters from the left. About two miles after this junction a long grade of about seven-tenths of a mile begins. Stop occasionally for resting, and viewing Zachs Cliffs, Long Beach, Squibnocket Pond, and other sights.

At South Rd. turn left. The road soon crests, then continues its up and down formations, continuing to snake around as well. At the sign LOBSTERVILLE TOWN BEACH turn right onto Lobsterville Rd. (there once was a fishing community here of this name). Enjoy a great downhill ride here as you head toward

113

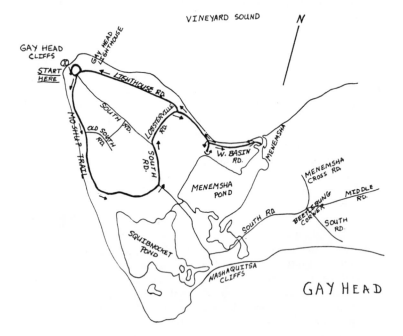

How to get there: From Vineyard Haven or elsewhere on the Island, go west on major roads following signs to Gay Head.

Vineyard Sound. In a little over a mile, Lighthouse Rd. joins you from the left, but you continue straight ahead and then bear left on West Basin Rd. Follow this road to its end, with Vineyard Sound on your left and Menemsha Pond on your right. An Adriatic-like pebbly beach is all along this road amid sand dunes. Directly ahead at the end of the road is Menemsha Bight, an inlet of the Sound.

You face the village of Menemsha across the Bight, but you can't get there from here. (Visit the hamlet on the West Tisbury-Menemsha ride.) Menemsha's harbor is beautifully protected and so is full of fishing and pleasure craft year round.

Turn around and head back up West Basin Rd. Take a brief detour down to the Pond's edge and the public landing when you come upon a road going off to the left. Return to West Basin Rd. and proceed straight ahead to its intersection with Lobsterville and Lighthouse Rd. Turn right and head west on Lighthouse Rd. Summer houses also dot the terrain on this side of Gay Head. After about two miles on Lighthouse Rd. you'll arrive at the Gay Head Lighthouse, built in 1952. The first lighthouse on this site was built in 1799. Continue to the Gay Head Cliffs and the end of the ride.

28.   Nantucket Town—Surfside

Number of miles: 10.2
Approximate pedalling time: 2 hours
Terrain: Flat to moderately hilly
Surface: Good to excellent
Things to see: The marvelous town of Nantucket itself, the Peter Foulger Museum, the Whaling Museum, Surfside Beach, Old Mill, Hawden-Satler House, and the Wharves

Start at Steamboat Wharf where the ferry comes in. There are two bike shops here in case you need supplies or repairs or want to rent a bike. Go up Broad St. past Easy St. (which is one-way coming from your left). Ride past Beach St., the Peter Foulger Museum and the Whaling Museum. A visit to both these museums is definitely in order for a clearer understanding of Nantucket's past.

Turn left on S. Water St. and then right on Main St. Main is paved with small, irregular cobblestones dating from the 1830s. These stones had served as ballast; they were laid to prevent wagons laden with oil casks from sinking into the sand. They were a boon in the 1800s but they are a bane to cyclists today.

Go up Main St. to the bank and bear left. Where Gardner comes in from the right, Main St. goes 45° right, but you bear left on New Mill St., passing Vestal on the right. At the fork, bear left on New Mill, which is one way against you so walk your bike. The next street is Prospect; turn left. Watch for street signs. (Since the houses are built close together, down to the edge of the narrow sidewalks, the street signs are often hung on the sides of houses.)

At the fork, bear right onto S. Prospect St. and go about a quarter of a mile to the intersection of Prospect, Williams, Sparks and Atlantic Ave. (also called Surfside Rd.). The sign says HOSPITAL and SURFSIDE. Turn almost 90° right onto Atlantic. Within a half mile, you'll see a BIKE PATH sign. Cross over to it and enjoy a leisurely ride to Surfside Beach. It's a two and a half mile ride to

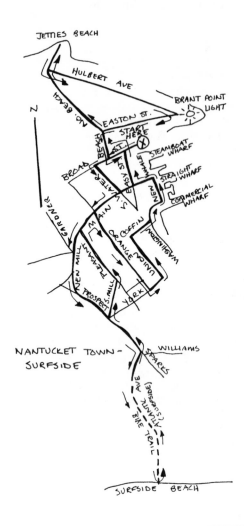

How to get there: Take the ferry from Woods Hole or Hyannis.

the beach, one of the Island's most popular, with lifeguard, snack bar, and bathhouse.

You can walk for miles in either direction along the South Shore here. After a surfeit of sun and surf, return along the same route to the Old Mill on the corner of S. Prospect, York, and S. Mill Sts.

Turn right around the site of the Old Mill onto S. Mill St. with the Mill on your left. This is the one survivor of the four which originally stood on the hill, grinding corn. Go downhill on S. Mill St. Turn left at the bottom of the hill at the "T" intersection with Pleasant St. Proceed along Pleasant St. to Main where you turn right. On the corner, at 96 Main St., is the Hawden Satler House. The three Georgian brick mansions across the street are identical. They were built between 1836 and 1838 by William Starbuck, a whaler, for his three sons. The middle house is still inhabited by descendants of the original owner. A Starbuck whaling ship set two records in 1859: It returned with 6,000 barrels of oil after a five year voyage!

At Orange St. turn right. There may not be a sign for Orange St. but there will be a series of sign posts reading: SURFSIDE-BIKE PATH; POLPIS-WAUWINET; HOSPITAL-AIRPORT and SIASCONSET BIKE PATH. Go as far as York St., just past Dover. More houses of whaling ship captains line Orange St. than any other street in the world. Go left on Union St. and head back toward the center of town. At Coffin St. turn right and go to Washington. Turn left, then immediately right heading toward Commercial ("Swain's") Wharf.

Lock your bike to any handy post here and walk around the three public wharves, Commercial, Straight and Old South. Commercial fishing and scalloping boats come and go, as do sail and motor boats of all descriptions.

From here proceed around the parking area on New Whale St., turn up Main, and then go along Easy St. four short blocks to Broad. If you have time for a swim, turn left on Broad and then right onto S. Beach St. Go three blocks to the stop sign at Easton St. Jog across to N. Beach St. Head up a slight hill. Beyond the Bird Sanctuary on the left, bear right where the sign says JETTIES BEACH, the main public beach on the Island. There is a gently sloping beach on one side and a shallow beach for children on the

119

other. The water here is warmer than most of New England. There is a lifeguard, bathhouse, and restaurant.

Leaving Jetties Beach, take the first left, Hulbert Ave. Follow it to Brant Pt. Light. Go right out to the point. Come back and continue straight ahead on Easton to the intersection with N. and S. Beach Sts. Turn left onto S. Beach and proceed back to Steamboat Wharf, your starting place.

29. Madaket

Number of miles: 15.7
Approximate pedalling time: 2 hours
Terrain: Flat to gently rolling
Surface: Very good
Things to see: The western end of Nantucket with its moors,
    Dionis Beach, Madaket Harbor and Beach, Hither Creek, Eel
    Point

Start this ride in front of the Peter Foulger Museum on Broad St.
Turn left on S. Water St., to Main St. A sign here points the way to
Madaket which is at the western end of the Island. Continue out
Main St. which becomes Madaket Rd., a paved road that curves left
and right and has a rolling grade. Two miles out from the Civil War
Monument is Eel Point Rd. and a sign reading DIONIS BEACH.
Turn right here. Once again you are crossing a tree-less heath.

Within three-quarters of a mile you come to a dirt road leading
off to the right to DIONIS BEACH. This beach has beautiful sand
dunes, a lifeguard, rest rooms and gentle surf (since it is on Nantucket Sound). When you're ready, come back to Madaket Rd. and
turn right.

Proceed across the heath (or moor as the Islanders call it). In
about two miles cross over an inlet between the two halves of Long
Pond, then pass Warren's Landing Rd. on the right. Within a mile
you'll come to Oakland Rd. on the right. Take this down to the
water and then turn left. Go as far as you can and turn left again,
back up to Madaket Rd. where you turn right. Within three quarters of a mile you come to Madaket Beach which is on the Atlantic
side, another splendid beach.

When you come back from the beach turn left and go across
the little bridge over the westernmost end of Hither Creek to
Smith Point on the left or Jackson Point on the right. Come back to
Madaket Rd. and turn left. When you come to a sign saying
HITHER CREEK BOATYARD turn left. This is Cambridge St. and
it takes you to Little Neck, a Nantucket Conservation Foundation

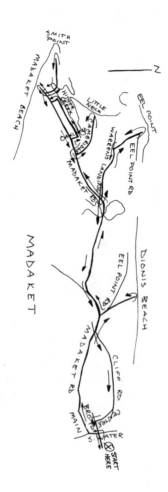

How to get there: Take the ferry from Woods Hole or Hyannis to Nantucket Town.

property open to the public. After exploring this lovely spot, return to Madaket Rd. once more and turn left.

If you have time, you can turn left when you come to Warren's Landing Rd. and take this dirt road out one and a half miles to Eel Point. When you hit the fork with Eel Point Rd. bear right onto Eel Pt. Rd. Eel Point is a 128 acre wildlife reservation where you can bird watch, fish, or swim. Coming back to Madaket Rd., turn left once more.

In just under two miles you turn left off Madaket onto Cliff Rd., just after the road to DIONIS BEACH. Cliff will take you back to Nantucket. Follow it as it curves around to the right and downhill to a fork; bear right, past Lilly St. on the right. This is now Centre St. Take it down to Broad St. Turn left and come back to your starting place.

30. Siasconset

Number of miles: 26.0 or 22.5
Approximate pedalling time: 2 hours, 45 minutes
Terrain: Flat to moderately hilly
Surface: Good to poor
Things to see: Nantucket Harbor, Wauwinet, Sankaty Head
Light, Siasconset, and Siasconset Beach

Start this ride at the foot of Main St. in front of the Pacific Club. In 1859, a group of former whaling ship captains who had sailed the Pacific formed the club for "yarning" together.

Walk up the square (because of the cobblestones); just before reaching the Pacific National Bank turn left onto Orange St. There may not be an "Orange St." sign but there will be a series of sign posts reading: SURFSIDE-BIKE PATH; POLPIS-WAUWINET; HOSPITAL-AIRPORT and SIASCONSET BIKE PATH. The latter is the destination for which you are heading. About one mile from the start, you will come to the Milestone Rotary identified by a sign: POLPIS SIASCONSET. Go around to the left and onto the Milestone Bike Path which starts here. This path will take you straight down to the only other town on Nantucket, Siasconset, called Sconset for short. The bike path is six miles long, most of it gently downhill.

You are now getting your first look at Nantucket's open heath or moor with its great variety of wildflowers, bayberry, scrub oaks, pine groves, and purple scotch heather. The first settlers found a tree-less island. The Coffin brothers imported 30,000 pine trees in 1851 and planted them in these outlying areas. About a half mile after the bike path ends you will come to a rotary that is distinguished by a flagpole made from a ship's spar. Here you go around to the right, uphill on Ocean Ave., also called Beach Rd. which goes along a bluff overlooking the Atlantic Ocean. On the right side are Nantucket's larger summer homes. The view to the left is spectacular! You can ride out as far as the Coast Guard Loran

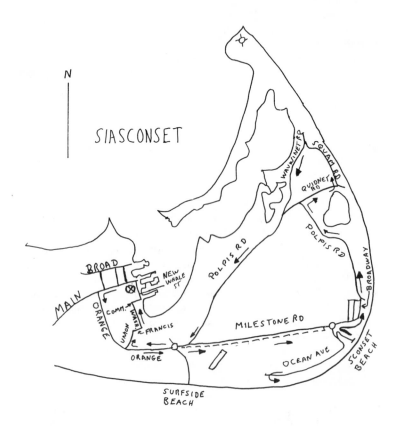

How to get there: Take the ferry to Nantucket from Woods Hole or Hyannis.

Station before turning around or you can turn around whenever you like and come back. Just before the rotary take a hairpin turn downhill and around to the right under the footbridge to Sconset Beach. There are bike racks and miles of beach stretching in either direction.

When you have picnicked or just rested, come back under the footbridge to the rotary where you will turn right and go into the village of Sconset with its doll-sized cottages. These were originally fishing shacks which were enlarged to their present size when the women of the fishermen decided to join them here. Turn left on Broadway to the "Y" with Polpis and head north. Continue on Polpis Rd. for about two and a half miles, past Sesachacha Pond on the right, until Polpis Rd. "Ts" into Quidnet Rd. Turn right onto Quidnet. (If you are getting tired or hungry—or both—you can cut 3½ miles off this ride by continuing left on Polpis Rd.) In just about a mile you will come to a sandy dirt road coming in from the left. This is Squam Rd. Turn left; ride one and a half miles on this narrow dirt/sand road, with the ocean on your right and Squam swamp on your left. It is a bit tricky on high pressure narrow width tires but it is navigable. It will bring you out onto Wauwinet Rd. with the Refuge Reception Station a short distance to the right. Ride down to the Station and ride or walk the short distance to the beach.

Come back onto Wauwinet Rd. as it rolls up and down for two miles until it "Ts" into Polpis Rd. Bear right onto Polpis and ride through the moors for four and a half miles until you come to Milestone Rd. About one mile before this intersection you will pass the Life Saving Museum, a replica of the first Life Saving Station built in 1874. Turn right onto Milestone Rd. You can cross over to the other side of Milestone and ride on the bike path if you prefer, up to the rotary where you turn right on Orange St. When you get to Union St., turn right and follow it around to Francis St. Turn right and then left onto Washington, which skirts South Beach.

At the point where Washington bears left at the fork with Candle St., Washington becomes one way against you. Turn 90° right onto Commercial (or Swain's) Wharf just before the fork, and then left on New Whale to tour the wharf area before ending your ride.

Safety

Riding the roads of Cape Cod and the islands on a bicycle can be dangerous—if you are careless with your equipment or with yourself. Observe all Massachusetts State bicycle laws. Obey all traffic signs, lights and other regulations. Ride with traffic staying close to the right. Give clear hand signals. Yield to pedestrians. Ride single file. Don't ride on sidewalks in town centers. Walk your bike when going against traffic on a one-way street. Call out and slow down when approaching horses. Check your bike before you leave. Make sure that all nuts are tight and that the derailleurs and brakes are working properly. No matter how long you have been riding use a check list before each ride. The one that we use is printed below.

Check List

1. Brakes
2. Derailleurs
3. Wheel nuts
4. Tires
5. Light
6. Reflector
7. Bolt-cutter-proof lock
8. Tool kit
9. Rag
10. Front and rear bag
11. First aid kit
12. Head protection
13. Sunglasses
14. Insect repellent
15. Wash-N-Dry towelettes
16. Toilet paper
17. Picnic ground cloth
18. Food
19. Water bottle
20. Towel and bathing suit
21. Watch
22. Money
23. *Short Bike Rides on Cape Cod*